he has refused his assent to laws the most wholesome and necessary for the public good:

he has forbidden his governors to pass laws of immed[illegible] unless suspended in their operation till his assent [illegible] and when so suspended, he has utterly neglected ~~utterly~~ to attend to them.

he has refused to pass other laws for the accomodation of large districts of people unless those people would relinquish the right of representation in the legislature, a right inestimable to them, & formidable to tyrants only:

he has dissolved Representative houses repeatedly & continually [illegible] manly firmness his invasions on the rights of the people:

~~[illegible]~~, he has refused for a long ~~space of time~~ time after such dissolutions to cause others to be elected, ~~[illegible]~~ legislative powers, incapable of annihilation, have ~~returned~~ to the people at large for their exercise, the state remaining in the mean time exposed to all the dangers of invasion from without, & convulsions within:

he has endeavored to prevent the population of these states; for that purpose obstructing the laws for naturalization of foreigners; refusing to pass others to encourage their migrations hither; & raising the conditions of new appropriations of lands:

he has [suffered the administration of justice totally to cease in some of these states] refusing his assent to laws for establishing judiciary powers:

he has made [our] judges dependant on his will alone, for the tenure of their offices, and the amount & payment of their salaries:

he has erected a multitude of new offices [by a self-assumed power, & sent hither swarms of officers to harrass our people & eat out their substance:

he has kept among us in times of peace standing armies [& ships of war] without the consent of our legislatures:

he has affected to render the military independent of & superior to the civil power:

he has combined with others to subject us to a jurisdiction foreign to our constitutions and unacknoleged by our laws; giving his assent to their acts of pretended ~~acts~~ of legislation, for quartering large bodies of armed troops among us;

for protecting them by a mock-trial from punishment for any murders which ~~they~~ should commit on the inhabitants of these states;

for cutting off our trade with all parts of the world;

for imposing taxes on us without our consent;

for depriving us of the benefits of trial by jury in many cases;

for transporting us beyond seas to be tried for pretended offences:

for abolishing the free system of English laws in a neighboring province, establishing therein an arbitrary government and enlarging it's boundaries so as to render it at once an example & fit instrument for introducing the same [illegible]

UNTO THE GENERATIONS

Daniel L. Marsh

UNTO THE GENERATIONS

The Roots of True Americanism

THE LONG HOUSE, INC.
Publishers
NEW CANAAN CONNECTICUT

1968

The LONG HOUSE, Inc.
PUBLISHERS
NEW CANAAN, CONNECTICUT
06840

LIBRARY OF CONGRESS CATALOG CARD NO. 68-27392

PRINTED AND BOUND IN THE UNITED STATES OF AMERICA

DESIGNED BY EUGENE M. ETTENBERG

EDITED BY JOHN HOWLAND SNOW

JACKET PHOTOGRAPH BY CAROL RUTH SHEPHERD

Preface

FOLLOWING the first world war, it seemed to me that the patriotism which had been generated for and by that war took all sorts of peculiar forms.

The situation throughout the Nation furnished abundant evidence that in the political realm no less than in the physical, action and reaction eventually are equal. Some sincere patriots became so zealous in their defense of what they felt was essential to the safeguarding of America that they manifested a spirit that was, in effect, actually un-American. On the other hand, certain persons who were open or secret disciples of communist or fascist doctrines took advantage of a widespread confusion and disseminated un-Americanism under the guise of liberal Americanism. Intolerance and bigotry were present in both groups. Name-calling became a fashion. Men and women grew hysterical, and proscribed and persecuted those with whom they did not agree, and impugned their motives and tarred them with the brutal stick of opprobrium. Professionals appeared, persons who affected the livery of patriotism for the sake of personal or political preferment. Many of the very elect were deceived.

I felt, as I am certain others did, the need of something that would give us some definitive distinctions by which all could measure reasonably the essence of true American patriotism. Surely, somewhere, there were documents that all could accept as the undisputed creed, or "bible", of what our Country stood for. So, on my own account, I began a study of the question and its implications. In odds and ends of time, and over a period of years, I made a comparative study of great American pronouncements of one kind or another, sifting them out by a testing process even as it seemed to me the ancient scholars might have tested other writings when they were determining which ones finally should be included in the New Testament.

When the second world war burst upon humanity I thought I would use the gist of my findings as my Baccalaureate Sermon to the graduating class of Boston University. Those who thronged Symphony Hall, and the multitude who listened to the Sermon over the radio, showed an eager and earnest appreciation of the point of view expressed. The attention given to the message by the public press, not only in the news columns but on the editorial pages, seemed to indicate that the study had indeed been timely. I became encouraged to expand the Baccalaureate Sermon by condensing the results of years of study into a book. A year later *The American Canon* was published by the Abingdon Cokesbury Press.

The book was extended a cordial reception, and was widely read. It went through many printings, and was translated into Spanish and distributed by the Department of State throughout South America. It also was rendered into Braille for the blind. As the years went on *The American Canon* went out of print.

Almost a generation later conditions throughout the Country became in many ways parallel to those of the 1930s, only now they had truly become alarming. Our systems of government—local, State and national—were honeycombed with corruption and malfeasance, and sinister legislation was being bought and paid for by those whom it would benefit. Vice and crime of every sort were transmuting our urban and rural thoroughfares into labyrinths of danger. It is hardly necessary to further recite the obvious.

A number of people approached me with the thought that my earlier book be republished, and in an enlarged edition. The idea appealed to me, and for reasons similar to those which had prevailed thirty years before. Perhaps such a book would be of service, even an inspiration, as was its predecessor. Perhaps it would help in re-evoking the lambent *spirit* of this Land, for here are the roots of true Americanism, taken from a line of predecessors who spoke, truly, unto the generations.

Eight American documents have been selected as the basis

of the book. Let me list them, together with what I deem their appropriate Scriptural connotations:

1. The *genesis* of the American Republic is the Mayflower Compact. In the beginning was the Pilgrim colony, with that positive, original, social Compact which is the legitimate source of all government.

2. Our *exodus* is the Declaration of Independence. That immortal document marks the going out of the American people from tyrannical bondage to the promised land of liberty and self-government.

3. Our *book of the law* is the Constitution of the United States, and the Ten Commandments have their counterpart in the political history of America as our Bill of Rights. In the Old Testament the Ten Commandments uttered their "Thou shalt not's" to individuals. The American people, in their first ten amendments, issued "Thou shalt not's" to their government.

4. We have our major and minor *prophecies*, the greatest of them all being Washington's Farewell Address. That thundering prophecy bears a relationship to the people of America comparable to that of the utterances of Isaiah and Jeremiah to the ancient Hebrews.

5. Our regional *psalms* are numerous; but *The Star-Spangled Banner*, the psalm of all the Nation, bespeaks our feelings even as the greatest of the psalms of David bespoke those of the people who first sang them.

6. The *gospel* of true Americanism was uttered by Abraham Lincoln, the savior of America, in his Second Inaugural Address. It was good news when it was first delivered; it is good news today.

7. We have our *epistles*, the greatest of them being the last thing Woodrow Wilson ever wrote. His THE ROAD AWAY FROM REVOLUTION will endure as long as our great system endures, a vision and a judgment of the historian who possessed the clearest insight and the finest analytical mind of any President in the history of America.

8. And finally, the *revelation*, Douglas MacArthur's address to his countrymen from the deck of the battleship *Missouri* at the formal surrender of Japan.

May the youth of America, enrolled in public and private schools, active in the troops of Girl and Boy Scouts, in Little Leagues, with the Campfire Girls, the 4-H Clubs, and among the almost countless organizations that are devoted to the well-being and ultimate citizenship of our young men and women, become familiar not only with the documents here presented but with the stories of how they came in being, of the immortal persons who composed them; and may they come to know and appreciate truly the abiding thoughts and scriptures which form the finest of our common heritage.

And in these days may there grow, within our youthful manhood, the kind of patriotism that Adlai Stevenson once defined: "A patriotism that puts country ahead of self; a patriotism which is not short, frenzied outbursts of emotion, but the tranquil and steady dedication of a lifetime."

May those who so soon will face the magnificent challenge which history has imposed upon them, meet it well.

Daniel Webster, on one occasion, looked back on history and said: "The past, at least, is secure." And now, as we of the maturer generations look toward those who will succeed us, let us pray that in their futures they may say to *their* children, with quiet pride: "The *future* is secure."

St. Petersburg, Florida — DANIEL L. MARSH
April, 1968

Contents

Plates

The Appendix

Foreword

THE SOCIETY in which we live is coming apart at the seams. A projection of the trends in public conduct presents the cruel spectre of an every-man-for-himself, might-makes-right national community in the years ahead. Thoughtful people must ponder the causes of this disintegration, and must find the persuasive reasons and the practical techniques which will restore order and purpose to our corporate living. *Unto the Generations* is the perfect primer for those who would engage in that endeavor.

Our high level of literacy is by itself a flimsy guaranty of the permanence of our institutions or, indeed, for confidence that they are being served by the breadth and depth of judgment that is now required. By their very character, those institutions can be sustained only as citizens truly understand the *nature* of their government and assume the obligations which it demands.

The wise and perceptive political philosopher, Montesquieu, observed that a form of government can operate only as long as the people behave in a manner which is suited to it. A dictatorship can last while the people are fearful. A monarchy endures as long as the people are loyal to the crown. And the life of a representative republic is limited or extended according to the virtue of the people.

The documents in this book are without meaning except to a virtuous people. Each of them can be ridiculed by the cynic, refuted by the sophist, or rejected by the tyrant. To the man who cares about his fellow man, however, and who genuinely wishes him justice in this life, their unfailing wisdom speaks with a sure power and clarity. No citizen who loves freedom is truly literate while unfamiliar with these writings.

Presented together as they are, they bear a further message:

Throughout the almost two centuries of the life of the Republic those who have given us our noblest leadership in word and deed have schooled themselves assiduously in the humanities. The authors of these documents did not achieve wisdom or clarity of thought and expression by experience only, they read and studied long and deeply about man's nature and man's purposes and man's failures and man's eternal glories. True leadership has always come from those who were conversant with man's utmost achievements, in action and in philosophy, and who had come to know the great literature which attends to the nature of man and the workings of his institutions.

Almost invariably, too, history's most constructive leadership has had a spiritual dimension. And it is significant that Chancellor Marsh has seen this, and organized his work in Biblical sequence. Here are giants of American history, men who not only led our Nation through times of stress, but lived their religious faith, and earnestly and humbly sought to do their utmost for the lasting good of their fellow beings.

The thoughts and judgments of such men come to us from man's illimitable heritage of the humanities, the inexhaustible wellspring from whose source we must draw the wisdom and the strength to meet the crises of our times. In pressing forward toward the fulfillment of the American dream, few works can help us chart the course more surely than *Unto the Generations.*

Rockford, Illinois
April, 1968

John Addison Howard
President, Rockford College

In ye name of god Amen· We whose names are underwriten,
the loyall subjects of our dread soveraigne Lord King James
by ye grace of god, of great Britaine, franc, & Ireland king
defender of ye faith, &c
Haveing undertaken, for ye glorie of god, and advancemente
of ye christian faith and honour of our king & countrie, a voyage to
plant ye first Colonie in ye Northerne parts of Virginia· Doe
by these presents solemnly & mutualy in ye presence of god, and
one of another; covenant, & combine our selves togeather into a
civill body politick; for our better ordering, & preservation & fur=
therance of ye ends aforesaid; and by vertue hearof to enacte,
constitute, and frame shuch just & equall lawes, ordinances,
acts, constitutions, & offices, from time to time, as shall be thought
most meete & convenient for ye generall good of ye Colonie: unto
which we promise all due submission and obedience· In witnes
wherof we have hereunder subscribed our names at Cap=
Codd ye ·11· of November, in ye year of ye raigne of our soveraigne
lord king James of England, france, & Ireland ye eighteenth
and of Scotland ye fiftie fourth. An: Dom· 1620·

by these presents solemnly & mutualy in ye presence of God, and one of another, covenant, & combine our selves togeather into a Civill body politick; for our better ordering, & preservation & furtherance of ye ends aforesaid; and by vertue hearof to enacte,

The Mayflower Compact

[1]

THE MAYFLOWER COMPACT, the genesis of our American Republic, had its own beginnings far back of its actual composition. Conditions were being prepared for it through hundreds of years before the Pilgrims left England, and during the clash of warfare which resulted from the Protestant Reformation. The Treaty of Augsburg brought that conflict to a temporary end in 1555, and the right of Protestantism to exist was recognized. But unfortunately, each state or principality received the power to control a creed within its borders. The head of a state thus was able to establish a church and to forbid his subjects to depart from its worship. Henry VIII of England, among others, took to himself the right to define the faith of his subjects and to control their consciences.

Some progress away from the arrogant supremacy of the state was made, through vicissitudes, for a century following. Finally there developed within the Established Church of England a group who were opposed to regal supremacy over a people's faith, and who were in favor of democratizing the Church and of purifying its ritual. Hence they came to be known as Puritans. The more bitter the persecution of the Puritans by the entrenched High Church party, the more insistent and persistent the Puritans became for the freedom of their worship. The lines of the movement tightened more and more, so that they came to stand not only for the simplification of church government and the abolition of empty formalities and a disgraceful worldliness, they reached for a superior sanctity of life. Most of them were to remain in the Church to purify it, but the more ardent minds, despairing of remodeling the Established Church from within, became Separatists.

One of the few small Separatist communities was at Scrooby, a little hamlet in middle England. It was the center of a tenant farming section, undistinguishable from many others. But in 1606 this little group determined to "shake off the yoke of anti-Christian bondage," and "joined themselves by a Covenant of the Lord, into a Church Estate . . . whatsoever it should cost them, the Lord assisting them."

The tiny congregation worshiped secretly in Scrooby Manor House, the keeper of which was William Brewster, the father of the William Brewster, Jr., who was to become the famous Elder Brewster of the Pilgrim colony of Massachusetts. From the little village of Austerfield, within walking distance, came too the youthful William Bradford, later the great Governor of the Colony of Massachusetts Bay.

No sooner were they discovered worshiping in the Manor House chapel than persecutions began by sanction of the ecclesiastical authorities of Yorkshire. Some, wrote Bradford, were "taken and clapt up in prison," and others had their "houses besett and watcht night and day and hardly escaped their hands."

By the autumn of 1607 the persecution had become so intolerable that they determined to go to Holland. But the King, equally determined that such migrations should not take place, ordered the ports closed against all who did not have the royal license to go. Thus, as Bradford remarks—to us it seems so quaintly—"Though they could not stay, yet they were not suffered to go." Nevertheless they went, by one means or another, from various ports, a few at a time, suffering all manner of hardships and embarrassments, until, through this process of unconscious winnowing, more than a hundred men, women, and children were gathered at Amsterdam by August of 1608, "armed with faith and patience."

Amsterdam was a liberal and progressive city; but, because of the general worldliness and presence of many heresies, it proved a disappointing refuge for the Pilgrims. Within a year, they moved to Leyden, about twenty-two miles to the southwest. While some of them pursued trades that furnished good training for their future life in distant Plymouth, for the most part they were doomed to rude and ill-paid toil. They did not wish their children to become Dutch, nor to be denied an opportunity for education. They disapproved of the sordid encroachments of the world upon the purity of their creed and practice. And they determined to seek a home where their faith and nationality would remain unimpaired.

After much discussion, they voted to go on to America. Financially unable to equip a ship and establish a colony, they sought help from the Virginia Company of London and the Virginia Company of Plymouth, two of the groups of Adventurers, as they were called, which were organized in England to finance and outfit colonial enterprises. They entered into partnership with the Adventurers to form a voluntary joint-stock company. It was a critical and momentous decision which those Pilgrims made; for trying as was reality in the New World, psychologically the anticipation of it was worse. They were terrified at the wild stories they heard of the dangers of shipwreck, the absence of sanitation at sea, and the famine, the nakedness, and the want they would face when their voyage ended. They were told that savage Indians flayed men with the shells of fishes, and cut off human steaks and chops, which they then broiled upon the coals before the victims' eyes. Bradford states in simple eloquence their intrepid answer to these forebodings: "It was answered that great and honorable actions are accompanied with great difficulties, and must be both enterprised and overcome with answerable courage."

It was evident that only a part of the Separatist Church could migrate. So they selected eighty or ninety from among the volunteers, having due regard for age and physical fitness. The whole little Church joined in hastening preparations for their departure. Properties were sold, goods donated, money collected. The equipment of tools, foodstuffs, and other supplies displayed their good common sense.

The plans called for increasing the original Pilgrim band

by recruits from England, with the simultaneous sailing of the Leyden group on the *Speedwell*, from Holland, and a second group on the *Mayflower*, from England. The two parties were to merge and organize at Southampton, from which port they were to proceed to America with both ships.

One delay followed another, so that it was near the end of July in 1620 before the Leyden Separatists kept their farewell fast, with sermon and the Holy Communion. Bradford writes with the unconscious eloquence of restraint: "So they left that goodly and pleasant city which had been their resting place near twelve years; but they knew they were Pilgrims, and looked not much on those things, but lifted up their eyes to the heavens, their dearest country, and quieted their spirits."

The *Mayflower* and *Speedwell* set sail from Southampton on August 15th. They had not gone far before the *Speedwell*'s captain said she was unseaworthy, and the two ships put in at Dartmouth. Again they were scarcely at sea when a second alarm was raised by the captain of the *Speedwell*, and they stood in at Plymouth. They ever after believed that the captain and the sailors of the *Speedwell* regretted their agreement, and had so crowded the ship with canvas that she sprung a leak. At Plymouth, they unloaded her, transferred much of the cargo to the *Mayflower*, weeded out the hesitant from both ships, and crowded one hundred and two willing and worthy men and women onto the tiny *Mayflower*. On the 16th of September, 1620, the good ship made her third and final departure—and sailed into a renown which became immortal.

The delays in getting started foredoomed the Pilgrims to land on a bleak New England shore in the midst of winter. They saw the land of England fade from sight on September 16, and saw nothing but the heaving sea until daybreak of November 20. They thought they were headed for the mouth of the Hudson, but the land which they sighted that morning was Cape Cod. When the captain attempted to turn the *Mayflower* southward he ran afoul the shoals which lay outside the Cape, and because of the lateness of the season and the roughness of the weather he turned about and put into Cape Cod harbor, off what now is Provincetown. Here they decided that the more hardy men-folk should explore the neighborhood and find a place that might be suitable for settlement. This meant they were abandoning all chance of residence within the Virginia Company's territory, under the patent they prized so highly; for they were far to the north of the limits of the very patent under which they had sailed.

The next day, while the little ship lay at anchor in the shelter of Cape Cod, the leaders learned that certain members of the party, especially the recruits secured in London, were chafing under restraint and were boldly asserting that as soon as they stepped on shore there would be an end to all authority. For, said they, nobody has authority here—and they were right! The King, it is true, made a general claim to this whole territory; but he had delegated no power to the Pilgrims, or to anybody else. They had not even been authorized to enter the country where they now were!

But the leaders were equal to the emergency. Their decision came swift as lightning. If England had no government for them, they would form a government of their own. The men of the company were forthwith assembled in the cabin of the *Mayflower*; the situation was laid before them, and then and there the immortal Compact was drawn up and signed by forty-one of the forty-three adult males aboard. Since the two whose names are wanting died soon after, it is likely that they were too sick at the time to participate themselves in the discussions.

Of this Compact John Quincy Adams said, in 1802: "This is perhaps the only instance in human history of that positive, original social compact which speculative philosophers have imagined as the only legitimate source of government. Here was a unanimous and personal assent by all the individuals of the community to the association *by which they became a nation.* The settlers of all the former European colonies had contented themselves with the powers conferred upon them by their respective charters, without looking beyond the seal of the royal parchment for the measure of their rights and the rule of their duties. The founders of Plymouth had been impelled by the peculiarities of their situation to examine the subject with deeper and more comprehensive research."

That Compact, drafted "in the name of God," was the beginning of our American Republic. The Colony, of which it was to become the instrument of government, was founded "for the glory of God." The Pilgrims covenanted and combined themselves together to enact "just and equal laws," and they voluntarily pledged themselves to yield to these laws "all due submission and obedience."

The first act of the citizens of the new Commonwealth was to confirm John Carver as Governor until the next New Year's Day, which, according to their calendar, fell on March 23rd.

Two explorations of the Cape itself were made. A third coastal exploration, made in the shallop they had brought with them, took them to Plymouth harbor. On December 21st, an exploring party of eighteen men drove their shallop along, looking for a landing place, until they came to the one solitary rock on all that diluvial shore. It was the stepping-stone to a nation.

Five days later the *Mayflower* made her way into the harbor at Plymouth. The loneliness, the anguish, the hardships, the near starvation, the sickness, the deaths, the sorrows of the Pilgrim band that first winter, can scarcely be comprehended by us today. The ravages of what Bradford called the "general sickness" were awesome. Of the one hundred and two Pilgrims who came over on the *Mayflower,* fifty-one—just half the total number—died the first year. Of the twenty-four households, four were wiped out completely by the sickness, and only four families entirely escaped its infection. The devotion with which these people served one another during those times is beyond description, comprehension or praise.

The mortality left the colony in the hands of young men. Bradford was thirty-one; Winslow, twenty-five; Allerton, thirty-two; Miles Standish, thirty-six; John Howland was twenty-eight and John Alden, twenty-one.

Carver was re-elected in March, but died shortly after. Thereupon William Bradford was elected Governor. Until his death in 1657 Bradford was the very soul of the Colony. He was a truly great man. Concerning him, Cotton Mather wrote: "He was a person for study as well as action: and hence, notwithstanding the difficulties through which he passed in his youth, he attained unto a notable skill in languages. The Dutch tongue was become almost as vernacular to him as the English. The French tongue he could also manage. The Latin and Greek he had mastered. But the Hebrew he most of all studied. Because, he said, he would see with his own eyes the ancient Oracles of God in their native beauty. He was also well skilled in History, in Antiquity, and in Philosophy . . . . But the crown of all was, his holy, prayerful, watchful, and fruitful walk with God, wherein he was very exemplary."

Except for a few brief intervals not only was William Bradford Governor of the Colony for the rest of his life, but for a while he was secretary and treasurer as well, and at the same time ministered to the sick with his own hands and worked with the rest of the men as they toiled in the fields.

Terrible as were the sufferings of that first Plymouth winter, when in the spring the *Mayflower* set sail for England not a single one of those Pilgrims returned with her. Henry Wadsworth Longfellow speaks the words for us:

> O strong hearts and true! not one went
> back in the *May Flower*!
> No, not one looked back, who had
> set his hand to this plowing!

They stayed, and lived their own lives in their own way. They stayed, and were loyal to the Compact by which they had determined to govern themselves. Under it they held elections; enacted laws; punished those who violated them; made treaties with the Indians; abolished the commune-scheme with which they had started out; settled their own property question by purchasing the common stock from the Adventurers and distributing the land among themselves, the citizens, giving to them titles of private ownership; made Captain Miles Standish head of their military organization, and planted the first permanent independent settlement in the New World. They made of their commonwealth a place where initiative lay within themselves, and not with landlords, nobility or kings.

The Mayflower Compact was the fundamental law of their new State. It pointed the way to equal rights and common duties. It became one of mankind's immortal documents, a contribution to the civic thought of all the world. Under it the Pilgrim Colony was not intolerant or bigoted, nor was it unjust, or overly severe. The Pilgrims applied the Bible to common life in a practical way. They guaranteed religious liberty. They stressed the imperative of righteous character. They exhibited no sickly, simpering sentimentality toward indolence or crime. They had a social conscience that manifested itself in law, the means by which individual conduct is socially governed. They believed in God with passionate devotion. Their lives were God-centered. God was no mere figure of speech to those sturdy Pilgrim sires; nor to their wives; nor to their children.

In spite of the terrible hardships and their unspeakable suffering and losses, the Pilgrims stayed in their new-made home. They stayed because they saw the eternal in the temporal, and the invisible in the visible, and because among them the material was dominated by the spiritual.

> God had sifted three kingdoms to find
> the wheat for this planting,
> Then had sifted the wheat, as the living
> seed of a nation;
> So say the chronicles old, and such
> is the faith of the people!

They stayed, because they had found that for which they went in quest when the warning wind sighed through the lines and crosstrees of the tiny *Mayflower*, and they left behind them their native land, its history, and its throne; its Church, its gold, its worldly cheer; and the green mounds where their brave sires slumbered. The course of their ship had been set in a pathless sea. They had groped their way through fogs and storms, and mists and blinding rain, and calm. They had landed on a frozen shore, bleak and dread, but they were glad. And as they knelt in prayer the very snows seemed warm, and the flakes falling on their cheeks melted into tears of gratitude. Pioneers of true Americanism, they stayed, they conquered; they sowed their seed in the sacred soil of the rights of men, and garnered a goodly harvest.

Ay, call it holy ground,
  The soil where first they trod!
They have left unstained what there they found—
  Freedom to worship God!

In CONGRESS, July 4, 1776.

The unanimous Declaration of the thirteen united States of America,

When in the Course of human events, it becomes necessary for one people to dissolve the political bands which have connected them with another, and to mong the powers of the earth, the separate and equal station to which the Laws of Nature and of Nature's God entitle them, a decent respect to the opinions of mankind requires that they declare the causes which impel them to the separation. —— We hold these truths to be self-evident, that all men are created equal, that they are endowed by their Creator tain unalienable Rights, that among these are Life, Liberty and the pursuit of Happiness. — That to secure these rights, Governments are instituted among Men, deriving their just from the consent of the governed, — That whenever any Form of Government becomes destructive of these ends, it is the Right of the People to alter or to abolish it, and to institute new ent, laying its foundation on such principles and organizing its powers in such form, as to them shall seem most likely to effect their Safety and Happiness. Prudence, indeed, ate that Governments long established should not be changed for light and transient causes; and accordingly all experience hath shewn, that mankind are more disposed to suffer, while sufferable, than to right themselves by abolishing the forms to which they are accustomed. But when a long train of abuses and usurpations, pursuing invariably the same Object design to reduce them under absolute Despotism, it is their right, it is their duty, to throw off such Government, and to provide new Guards for their future security. — Such has patient sufferance of these Colonies; and such is now the necessity which constrains them to alter their former Systems of Government. The history of the present King of Great is a history of repeated injuries and usurpations, all having in direct object the establishment of an absolute Tyranny over these States. To prove this, let Facts be submitted to a candid d. —— He has refused his Assent to Laws, the most wholesome and necessary for the public good. —— He has forbidden his Governors to pass Laws of immediate sing importance, unless suspended in their operation till his Assent should be obtained; and when so suspended, he has utterly neglected to attend to them. —— He has refused to Laws for the accommodation of large districts of people, unless those people would relinquish the right of Representation in the Legislature, a right inestimable to them and formidable ts only. —— He has called together legislative bodies at places unusual, uncomfortable, and distant from the depository of their Public Records, for the sole purpose of fatiguing them into nce with his measures. —— He has dissolved Representative Houses repeatedly, for opposing with manly firmness his invasions on the rights of the people. —— He has refused for time, after such dissolutions, to cause others to be elected; whereby the Legislative powers, incapable of Annihilation, have returned to the People at large for their exercise; the State remain the mean time exposed to all the dangers of invasion from without, and convulsions within. —— He has endeavoured to prevent the population of these States; for that purpose obstruc Laws for Naturalization of Foreigners; refusing to pass others to encourage their migrations hither, and raising the conditions of new Appropriations of Lands. —— He has obstructed the stration of Justice, by refusing his Assent to Laws for establishing Judiciary powers. —— He has made Judges dependent on his Will alone, for the tenure of their offices, and the amount yment of their salaries. —— He has erected a multitude of New Offices, and sent hither swarms of Officers to harrass our people, and eat out their substance. —— He has kept among imes of peace, Standing Armies without the Consent of our legislatures. —— He has affected to render the Military independent of and superior to the Civil power. —— He has combined ers to subject us to a jurisdiction foreign to our constitution, and unacknowledged by our laws; giving his Assent to their Acts of pretended Legislation: — For Quartering large bodies of troops among us: — For protecting them, by a mock Trial, from punishment for any Murders which they should commit on the Inhabitants of these States: — For cutting off e with all parts of the world: — For imposing Taxes on us without our Consent: — For depriving us in many cases, of the benefits of Trial by Jury: — For transporting us beyond tried for pretended offences: — For abolishing the free System of English Laws in a neighbouring Province, establishing therein an Arbitrary government, and enlarging its Boundaries ender it at once an example and fit instrument for introducing the same absolute rule into these Colonies: — For taking away our Charters, abolishing our most valuable Laws, and fundamentally the Forms of our Governments: — For suspending our own Legislatures, and declaring themselves invested with power to legislate for us in all cases whatsoever. as abdicated Government here, by declaring us out of his Protection and waging War against us. —— He has plundered our seas, ravaged our Coasts, burnt our towns, and destroyed the lives ple. —— He is at this time transporting large Armies of foreign Mercenaries to compleat the works of death, desolation and tyranny, already begun with circumstances of Cruelty & perfidy aralleled in the most barbarous ages, and totally unworthy the Head of a civilized nation. —— He has constrained our fellow Citizens taken Captive on the high Seas to bear Arms against ntry, to become the executioners of their friends and Brethren, or to fall themselves by their Hands. —— He has excited domestic insurrections amongst us, and has endeavoured to bring on the s of our frontiers, the merciless Indian Savages, whose known rule of warfare, is an undistinguished destruction of all ages, sexes and conditions. In every stage of these Oppressions We itioned for Redress in the most humble terms: Our repeated Petitions have been answered only by repeated injury. A Prince, whose character is thus marked by every act which may define a Tyrant, to be the ruler of a free people. Nor have We been wanting in attentions to our Brittish brethren. We have warned them from time to time of attempts by their legislature to extend an unwarrant diction over us. We have reminded them of the circumstances of our emigration and settlement here. We have appealed to their native justice and magnanimity, and we have conjured them s of our common kindred to disavow these usurpations, which, would inevitably interrupt our connections and correspondence. They too have been deaf to the voice of justice and of inity. We must, therefore, acquiesce in the necessity, which denounces our Separation, and hold them, as we hold the rest of mankind, Enemies in War, in Peace Friends. ——

We, therefore, the Representatives of the united States of America, in General Congress, Assembled, appealing to the Supreme Judge of the world for the rectitude of our in do, in the Name, and by Authority of the good People of these Colonies, solemnly publish and declare, That these United Colonies are, and of Right ought to be Free and Independent that they are Absolved from all Allegiance to the British Crown, and that all political connection between them and the State of Great Britain, is and ought to be totally dissolved; and Free and Independent States, they have full Power to levy War, conclude Peace, contract Alliances, establish Commerce, and to do all other Acts and Things which Independent ay of right do. —— And for the support of this Declaration, with a firm reliance on the protection of divine Providence, we mutually pledge to each other our Lives, our Fortunes sacred Honor.

– Gwinnett
n Hall
Walton.

Wm Hooper
Joseph Hewes,
John Penn

Edward Rutledge 1.

Thos Heyward Junr.
Thomas Lynch Junr.
Arthur Middleton

John Hancock

Samuel Chase
Wm Paca
Thos Stone
Charles Carroll of Carrollton

George Wythe
Richard Henry Lee
Th Jefferson
Benj Harrison
Thos Nelson jr.
Francis Lightfoot Lee
Carter Braxton

Robt Morris
Benjamin Rush
Benj. Franklin
John Morton
Geo Clymer
Jas. Smith
Geo. Taylor
James Wilson
Geo. Ross
Caesar Rodney
Geo Read
Thos M:Kean

Wm Floyd
Phil. Livingston
Frans. Lewis
Lewis Morris

Richd Stockton
Jno Witherspoon
Fras. Hopkinson
John Hart
Abra Clark

Josiah Bartlett
Wm Whipple
Saml Adams
John Adams
Robt Treat Paine
Elbridge Gerry
Step. Hopkins
William Ellery
Roger Sherman
Samel Huntington
Wm Williams
Oliver Wolcott
Matthew Thornton

The Declaration of Independence

[2]

THE DECLARATION OF INDEPENDENCE, our exodus from human bondage, came out of a vast and noble courage. It does not require much space to write it, or much time to repeat it; but it was the final crown of years of political revolution.

The early settlements of America were made from different motives, and by people of varying racial inheritances. But no matter by whom the settlements originally were made, in time they all came into the possession of Great Britain.

As early as 1660 we find the specific beginnings of oppression. The British government passed and attempted to enforce the despised Navigation Acts. Then, in 1760, George III came to the throne. He was only twenty-two years old; he was dull, uneducated, intolerant, bigoted, and finally crazy. His mother had dinned into his ears the dictum: "George, be King!" He accepted the then common European idea that a colony existed only to enrich the mother country. He thought he saw in his American possessions a convenient source of revenue to help meet his war debts. Through Parliament, therefore, he began the collection of new taxes and the enforcement of the Navigation Acts. Commanders of British frigates were given royal authority to search American homes for smuggled goods.

Oppression followed oppression, insult was heaped upon

insult, injustice was added to injustice, until the elemental intelligence, character, and feeling in the Americans were ready to burst forth like a volcano. When Patrick Henry cried: "Is life so dear, or peace so sweet, as to be purchased at the price of chains and slavery?" he made articulate the overwhelming feeling in many an American breast.

A Continental Congress was called in September, 1774, to meet in Philadelphia. The declared purpose of this Congress was: "To consult on the present state of the colonies; and to deliberate upon wise and proper measures for the recovery of their just rights and liberties; and the restoration of union and harmony between Great Britain and the colonies, most ardently desired by all good men."

At this time the colonies were simply standing upon their rights as Englishmen. They sent a petition to the King and the King refused to receive it. A second Continental Congress was called, to meet in May, 1775, less than a month after the battles of Lexington and Concord. The Revolutionary War was on, and the Americans who had started out to "recover and establish the just rights and liberties of the colonies," soon discovered that vast new rights could be in store for them. By the summer of 1776 these new rights were being discussed in Philadelphia.

And so we come to the Declaration of Independence—the magnificent crystallization of the sentiment of the day. Yet Thomas Jefferson, the author of the Declaration, was accused by more than one of plagiarism in the writing of it. Certainly many of his contemporaries were saying things that influenced his thinking. But plagiarism? Jefferson was well aware of the rapidly growing sentiment for independence, and of the expressions of that sentiment that were taking place. Many historians, for instance, consider the Mecklenburg Declaration—made by militiamen of Mecklenburg County in North Carolina—to have been the first open challenge of American independence from Great Britain. The date, May 20, 1775, is inscribed on the official North Carolina flag, and its anniversary each year is a State holiday. Certainly the Mecklenburg incident, and many other indices of the people's thinking, were known to Jefferson and of course influenced greatly his own concept of what had to be said. John Dickinson, an influential leader from Pennsylvania, had published his cogent *Letters From a Farmer in Pennsylvania to the Inhabitants of the British Colonies.* Benjamin Franklin's pragmatic mind had marshaled the facts of history and philosophy to the support of his position that Parliamentary legislation for the colonies was "usurpation". Thomas Paine's pamphlet, *Common Sense,* exerted as great an influence upon the mind of America in 1776 as would Harriet Beecher Stowe's *Uncle Tom's Cabin* in the years preceding the Civil War.

In 1822, John Adams wrote a letter to Timothy Pickering, in which he said quite frankly, about the Declaration, "There is not an idea in it but what had been hacknied in Congress for two years before." Adams observed that the "natural rights" philosophy was a commonplace of the day and that the political crimes listed by Jefferson were known to all. Jefferson did not dispute the fact that the Declaration was "a commonplace compilation". He wrote later to James Madison:

> Pickering's observations, and Mr. Adam's in addition, "that it [the Declaration] contained no new ideas, that it is a common place compilation, it's sentiments hacknied in Congress for two years before, . . ." may all be true. Of that I am not to be the judge. Richard H. Lee charged it as copied from Locke's treatise on government. . . . I know only that I turned to neither book or pamphlet while writing it. I did not consider it as any part of my charge to invent new ideas altogether & to offer no sentiment which had ever been expressed before. . . .

If the Declaration had contained things that no one had thought of previously, the people undoubtedly would not have welcomed it. Nor would the Congress have adopted a declaration that contained either philosophy or history which they did not accept, and which the country as a whole did not understand. Jefferson, by a process of mental distillation, as it were, gathered up the inarticulate or half-expressed beliefs and aspirations of the day, and precipitated them in the cogent and unforgettable phrases of the Declaration of Independence. In writing to Richard Henry Lee, in 1825, Jefferson reaffirmed that he only attempted to express the ideas of the Whigs, who had no disagreement among themselves on the subject.

The truth is that the philosophy of the day might have lain submerged in the public mind, like some water-soaked log, had not the British government struck the steel of oppression upon the flint of America's burgeoning sense of freedom. The spark struck out; it kindled the land into burning heat, and the philosophy of the day took fire and came to blaze so brightly that it illuminated the whole human world.

When we come to the actual writing of the Declaration, we find this entry in the *Journals of The Continental Congress*, as of Friday, June 7, 1776, and in the handwriting of Charles Thompson, Secretary:

> Certain resolutions being moved & seconded Resolved That the consideration of them be referred till to morrow morning & that the members be enjoined to attend punctually at 10 o'clock in order to take the same into consideration.

The "Certain resolutions" declared that "these United Colonies are, and of right ought to be, free and independent States. . . ."

On June 11th a committee was appointed to prepare the Declaration itself; "The members chosen Mr Jefferson, Mr J Adams, Mr Franklin, Mr Shearman & Mr R. R. Livingston."

The member selected by his fellow committeemen to write the Declaration was Thomas Jefferson, a young man of thirty-three, from Virginia. He was a tall, charming, red-headed lawyer; a horseman, a scientist, a philosopher, a man of wealth and social position, an aristocrat-democrat. He was one of America's truly great men—one of our greatest. Jefferson was chosen to write the Declaration of Independence because, as John Adams said, he had "a reputation for literature, science, and a happy talent of composition. Writings of his were handed about remarkable for the peculiar felicity of expression."

Jefferson sat in the parlor of his second-floor lodgings in Philadelphia, at the corner of Seventh and Market Streets, and, without consulting a book or pamphlet, wrote in a half day's time the great symbol of our Nation's exodus. The first rough draft may be seen now in the Library of Congress. There are many corrections in it—words crossed out, and words written in. It is filled with interlining and marginal notes. Most of these emendations are in the handwriting of Jefferson himself.

After he had drafted the document, Jefferson submitted it to John Adams and Benjamin Franklin. Adams made two corrections, and Franklin, five. It was then submitted to the Committee, and approved without further change. Jefferson now made what he called a "fair copy" to use in making the Committee's report to Congress.

Forty-seven years later, in a letter to James Madison in 1823, Jefferson said:

> The Committee of 5 met, no such thing as a sub-committee was proposed, but they unanimously pressed on myself alone to undertake the draught. I consented; I drew it; but before I reported it to the committee I communicated it separately to Dr. Franklin and Mr. Adams requesting their corrections: . . . and you have seen the original paper now in my hands, with the corrections of Dr. Franklin and Mr. Adams interlined in their own handwriting. Their alterations were two or three only, and merely verbal. I then wrote a fair copy, reported it to the committee, and from them, unaltered to the Congress.

The draft was reported to Congress on June 28th. It was laid on the table until July 1st. On that day it was debated, and adopted by the Committee of the Whole. On the 2nd, a resolution of independence was adopted by Congress, and it was this Resolution, expressing the sense of the Continental Congress, that caused John Adams to write to his wife Abigail on the 3rd:

Yesterday the greatest question was decided which ever was debated in America, and a greater, perhaps, never was nor will be decided among men.

Sitting in the State House in Philadelphia, the Congress now proceeded to the consideration of the Jefferson draft as recommended by its membership sitting as a Committee of the Whole. The Declaration was considered on the 3rd, and adopted on the 4th.

Fifty-six names are appended to this immortal document. They represented every stratum of society, so far as society had become stratified in America at that time. For the most part the signers were well educated. They were men in the very strength and prime of manhood. They were neither foolish and impetuous youth nor old men in their dotage. The average age of the fifty-six signers was 44 years. Samuel Adams was 53 years old; John Hancock, 39; Richard Henry Lee, 44; Benjamin Harrison, 36; John Adams, 40; Thomas Jefferson, 33; Benjamin Franklin, 70; Roger Sherman, 55; Robert Livingston, 29.

The effect of the adoption of the Declaration of Independence was instant and epochal. It awakened joy throughout the entire land. It united the Colonies as nothing else on earth could have done. It changed a defensive war for the redress of wrongs into a war for the establishment of a new and separate government. It drew a clear-cut issue between those who were loyal to the newly formed government and those who remained loyal to the British crown. It moved the people to face hardship and privation for the cause of freedom, and prompted the soldiers to plunge with a new and dauntless pride into the crimson sea of carnage.

From 1776 to the present hour the Declaration of Independence has been the inspiration of a new hope among the oppressed of every tribe and nation throughout the world. Let persons in affluent circumstances try as they will to deny its dictum that "all men are created equal," still the poor and unfortunate and dispossessed will grasp at it as will drowning men at straws. Undoubtedly, what the Fathers of 1776 were trying to say was that under just government all men are equal in political privilege and political obligation. The Declaration says to all humanity that there is but one family picnicking on this right little, tight little playground of ours called the earth. Adam, or cave man, or Anthropoidea—it does not matter—the blood of the first man is in all our veins. And the Declaration of Independence is the Call of the Blood.

The Declaration's doctrine that governments derive their just powers from the consent of the governed has made for the spread of a hope of representative democracy throughout all the earth. Although the recrudescence of tyranny in the totalitarian State and the dictator is ever present before our eyes, yet wherever and whenever the Declaration's doctrine is known and becomes accepted, rulers can be no more than attorneys, agents, trustees, and servants of the people.

Its principles have buttressed religious toleration as well as political freedom. Charles Carroll, the only Roman Catholic to sign the Declaration, and the last of all the signers to die, wrote on February 20th, 1829, more than fifty-two years after his momentous act:

> When I signed the Declaration of Independence I had in view not only our independence of England, but the toleration of all sects professing the Christian religion, and communicating to them all equal rights. Happily this wise and salutary measure has taken place for eradicating religious feuds and persecution, and become a useful lesson to all governments.

As originally presented to Congress, the Declaration contained three references to God: the first in the opening paragraph, where "the Laws of Nature and of Nature's God" are invoked; the second in the paragraph following, where "We hold these truths to be self-evident, that all men . . . are endowed by their Creator with inherent and inalienable Rights" (which Congress amended to read "certain unalienable Rights"); and the third, where the signers, in their ultimate beseechment, appeal "to the Supreme Judge of the world for the rectitude of our intentions . . ."

The draft closed with these words of total dedication: "And, for the support of this Declaration, we mutually pledge to each other our Lives, our Fortunes, and our sacred Honor." Congress, by amendment, inserted after the word "Declaration" these ten words: "with a firm reliance on the protection of divine Providence".

America is the Messiah of nations. Her special mission is to be the hospice of freedom. She must guard the idea of Liberty, gently but indomitably, even as the never-sleeping dragon of mythology once guarded the garden of the Hesperides. We must make good. And while we live and die for our ideals we must forever honor and acknowledge the benign omnipotence of Almighty God.

We the People

of the United States, in Order to form a more perfect Union, establish Justice, insure domestic Tranquility, provide for the common defence, promote the general Welfare, and secure the Blessings of Liberty to ourselves and our Posterity, do ordain and establish this Constitution for the United States of America.

Article. I

Section. 1. All legislative Powers herein granted shall be vested in a Congress of the United States, which shall consist of a Senate and House of Representatives.

Section. 2. The House of Representatives shall be composed of Members chosen every second Year by the People of the several States, and the Electors in each State shall have the Qualifications requisite for Electors of the most numerous Branch of the State Legislature.

No Person shall be a Representative who shall not have attained to the Age of twenty five Years, and been seven Years a Citizen of the United States, and who shall not, when elected, be an Inhabitant of that State in which he shall be chosen.

Representatives and direct Taxes shall be apportioned among the several States which may be included within this Union, according to their respective Numbers, which shall be determined by adding to the whole Number of free Persons, including those bound to Service for a Term of Years, and excluding Indians not taxed, three fifths of all other Persons. The actual Enumeration shall be made within three Years after the first Meeting of the Congress of the United States, and within every subsequent Term of ten Years, in such Manner as they shall by Law direct. The Number of Representatives shall not exceed one for every thirty Thousand, but each State shall have at Least one Representative; and until such enumeration shall be made, the State of New Hampshire shall be entitled to chuse three, Massachusetts eight, Rhode Island and Providence Plantations one, Connecticut five, New York six, New Jersey four, Pennsylvania eight, Delaware one, Maryland six, Virginia ten, North Carolina five, South Carolina five, and Georgia three.

When vacancies happen in the Representation from any State, the Executive Authority thereof shall issue Writs of Election to fill such Vacancies.

The House of Representatives shall chuse their Speaker and other Officers; and shall have the sole Power of Impeachment.

Section. 3. The Senate of the United States shall be composed of two Senators from each State, chosen by the Legislature thereof, for six Years; and each Senator shall have one Vote.

Immediately after they shall be assembled in Consequence of the first Election, they shall be divided as equally as may be into three Classes. The Seats of the Senators of the first Class shall be vacated at the Expiration of the second Year, of the second Class at the Expiration of the fourth Year, and of the third Class at the Expiration of the sixth Year, so that one third may be chosen every second Year; and if Vacancies happen by Resignation, or otherwise, during the Recess of the Legislature of any State, the Executive thereof may make temporary Appointments until the next Meeting of the Legislature, which shall then fill such Vacancies.

No Person shall be a Senator who shall not have attained to the Age of thirty Years, and been nine Years a Citizen of the United States, and who shall not, when elected, be an Inhabitant of that State for which he shall be chosen.

The Vice President of the United States shall be President of the Senate, but shall have no Vote, unless they be equally divided.

The Senate shall chuse their other Officers, and also a President pro tempore, in the Absence of the Vice President, or when he shall exercise the Office of President of the United States.

The Senate shall have the sole Power to try all Impeachments. When sitting for that Purpose, they shall be on Oath or Affirmation. When the President of the United States is tried, the Chief Justice shall preside: And no Person shall be convicted without the Concurrence of two thirds of the Members present.

Judgment in Cases of Impeachment shall not extend further than to removal from Office, and disqualification to hold and enjoy any Office of honor, Trust or Profit under the United States: but the Party convicted shall nevertheless be liable and subject to Indictment, Trial, Judgment and Punishment, according to Law.

Section. 4. The Times, Places and Manner of holding Elections for Senators and Representatives, shall be prescribed in each State by the Legislature thereof; but the Congress may at any time by Law make or alter such Regulations, except as to the Places of chusing Senators.

The Congress shall assemble at least once in every Year, and such Meeting shall be on the first Monday in December, unless they shall by Law appoint a different Day.

Section. 5. Each House shall be the Judge of the Elections, Returns and Qualifications of its own Members, and a Majority of each shall constitute a Quorum to do Business; but a smaller Number may adjourn from day to day, and may be authorized to compel the Attendance of absent Members, in such Manner, and under such Penalties as each House may provide.

Each House may determine the Rules of its Proceedings, punish its Members for disorderly Behaviour, and, with the Concurrence of two thirds, expel a Member.

Each House shall keep a Journal of its Proceedings, and from time to time publish the same, excepting such Parts as may in their Judgment require Secrecy; and the Yeas and Nays of the Members of either House on any question shall, at the Desire of one fifth of those Present, be entered on the Journal.

Neither House, during the Session of Congress, shall, without the Consent of the other, adjourn for more than three days, nor to any other Place than that in which the two Houses shall be sitting.

Section. 6. The Senators and Representatives shall receive a Compensation for their Services, to be ascertained by Law, and paid out of the Treasury of the United States. They shall in all Cases, except Treason, Felony and Breach of the Peace, be privileged from Arrest during their Attendance at the Session of their respective Houses, and in going to and returning from the same; and for any Speech or Debate in either House, they shall not be questioned in any other Place.

No Senator or Representative shall, during the Time for which he was elected, be appointed to any civil Office under the Authority of the United States, which shall have been created, or the Emoluments whereof shall have been encreased during such time; and no Person holding any Office under the United States, shall be a Member of either House during his Continuance in Office.

Section. 7. All Bills for raising Revenue shall originate in the House of Representatives; but the Senate may propose or concur with Amendments as on other Bills.

Every Bill which shall have passed the House of Representatives and the Senate, shall, before it become a Law, be presented to the President of the

Article. VII.

The Ratification of the Conventions of nine States, shall be sufficient for the Establishment of this Constitution between the States so ratifying the Same.

The Word, "the," being interlined between the seventh and eighth Lines of the first Page, The Word "Thirty" being partly written on an Erazure in the fifteenth Line of the first Page, The Words "is tried" being interlined between the thirty second and thirty third Lines of the first Page and the Word "the" being interlined between the forty third and forty fourth Lines of the second Page.

Attest William Jackson Secretary

done in Convention by the Unanimous Consent of the States present the Seventeenth Day of September in the Year of our Lord one thousand seven hundred and Eighty seven and of the Independance of the United States of America the Twelfth In witness whereof We have hereunto subscribed our Names,

Go: Washington — Presidt. and deputy from Virginia

Delaware { Geo: Read, Gunning Bedford jun, John Dickinson, Richard Bassett, Jaco: Broom

Maryland { James McHenry, Dan of St Thos. Jenifer, Danl Carroll

Virginia { John Blair —, James Madison Jr.

North Carolina { Wm. Blount, Richd. Dobbs Spaight., Hu Williamson

South Carolina { J. Rutledge, Charles Cotesworth Pinckney, Charles Pinckney, Pierce Butler.

Georgia { William Few, Abr Baldwin

New Hampshire { John Langdon, Nicholas Gilman

Massachusetts { Nathaniel Gorham, Rufus King

Connecticut { Wm. Saml. Johnson, Roger Sherman

New York . . . Alexander Hamilton

New Jersey { Wil: Livingston, David Brearley., Wm. Paterson., Jona: Dayton

Pensylvania { B Franklin, Thomas Mifflin, Robt Morris, Geo. Clymer, Thos. FitzSimons, Jared Ingersoll, James Wilson, Gouv Morris

In Convention. Monday September 17th 1787.

Present

The States of

New Hampshire, Massachusetts, Connecticut, Mr. Hamilton from New York, New Jersey, Pennsylvania, Delaware, Maryland, Virginia, North Carolina, South Carolina and Georgia.

Resolved, That the preceeding Constitution be laid before the United States in Congress assembled, and that it is the Opinion of this Convention, that it should afterwards be submitted to a Convention of Delegates, chosen in each State by the People thereof, under the Recommendation of its Legislature, for their Assent and Ratification; and that each Convention assenting to, and ratifying the Same, should give Notice thereof to the United States in Congress assembled.

Resolved, That it is the Opinion of this Convention, that as soon as the Conventions of nine States shall have ratified this Constitution, the United States in Congress assembled should fix a Day on which Electors should be appointed by the States which shall have ratified the same, and a Day on which the Electors should assemble to vote for the President, and the Time and Place for commencing Proceedings under this Constitution. That after such Publication the Electors should be appointed, and the Senators and Representatives elected: That the Electors should meet on the Day fixed for the Election of the President, and should transmit their Votes certified, signed, sealed and directed, as the Constitution requires, to the Secretary of the United States in Congress assembled, that the Senators and Representatives should convene at the Time and Place assigned; that the Senators should appoint a President of the Senate, for the sole Purpose of receiving, opening and counting the Votes for President; and, that after he shall be chosen, the Congress, together with the President, should, without Delay, proceed to execute this Constitution.

By the unanimous Order of the Convention

W. Jackson Secretary.

Go: Washington Presidt.

and secure the Blessings of Liberty to ourselves and our Posterity

The Constitution of the United States

[3]

OUR BOOK of fundamental law is the Constitution of the United States. It has now been the fundamental law of America for one hundred and four score years. It is the oldest written constitution of any government, and the Republic of the United States of America is the oldest government under any written definition in the whole wide world.

The Constitution is a constant witness to the self-restraint which the American people of 1787 were so wise as to place upon themselves and their posterity.

Its philosophy did not spring Pallas-like from the brain of Jove. It was the crowning of a toilsome evolution of the ages. All the political strivings of the past—from Marathon, where the dauntless soldiers of ancient Hellas maintained the liberty of Athens, to Runnymede, where the English barons and yeomanry wrung from a tyrant King the Magna Carta—all these strivings are alive in our Republic today. As an instrument for the protection of human rights, our Constitution roots in and grows out of the heroic past of people, from the most remote antiquity.

The original recommendation for the "convening of a General Congress" was made by Benjamin Franklin in July, 1773. In fulfillment of his suggestion, as it was favorably received by a number of the Colonies, the first Continental Congress met in Philadelphia in September, 1774. The body was not a congress in the sense that it possessed legislative power. It was a conference of delegates from the Colonies who came together to discuss the grievances which they had against Great Britain, and to confer about methods which might redress those grievances peacefully. The Congress adjourned on October 26th, after providing for a further Congress if the crisis continued.

The Second Continental Congress met in 1775, and before it met the Battles of Lexington and Concord had been fought. Relative to the military engagements of history, these were the merest skirmishes; but the shot fired "By the rude bridge that arched the flood" at Concord was in very truth "heard round the world." When the first blood spilled for American independence soaked into the sod of Lexington Green it was as seed that grew and burst into the crimson bloom of fire, and courage, and eventually of benevolence. Nothing else could so effectively have made the colonists, all along the Atlantic seaboard, recognize the urgency of united effort as did Britain's use of arms against Americans who, up to this very moment, had regarded themselves as British.

From now until the end of the war the Continental Congress was the one symbol of the political unity of America. As a government it was impotent, even during the Revolution. It was headless. Such success as it had was due to the common fear of the Redcoats, and the spirit of cooperation which characterized the people—and to the subtle, quiet authority of George Washington. So far as the Congress was concerned, it possessed no powers other than persuasion. The result was pitiable inefficiency.

Articles of Confederation were adopted by Congress in 1781, near the close of the Revolution. The adoption of these Articles of Confederation marked the first, tenuous advance over the chaos which had obtained, but Congress, under the Articles of Confederation, still was utterly impotent. The country remained without an executive head. There really was no such thing as national authority. The most that you could say for the Articles of

Confederation was that they had constituted, out of thirteen separate and individual States, a league.

Forces of disintegration were at work from 1783 to 1787. A situation of general anarchy obtained. Credit was gone. Congress made recommendations to the different States concerning the raising of revenue, and the States treated the recommendations with contempt. Congress issued paper money, and citizens in derision plastered the walls of their houses with it. The army demanded pay, and Congress was unable to pay. The army was without discipline, and one detachment of disgruntled soldiers actually besieged the State House in Philadelphia, where the Congress itself was meeting. Congress thereupon fled to Princeton, New Jersey, and then to the city of New York, where it remained until after the Constitutional Convention. Now that the Redcoats were gone, the former Colonies, more than anything else, feared each other. Incipient rebellions were breaking out. Wise Americans like Washington and Franklin could foresee nothing but more disorder. Anarchy shook the land. Lawlessness was rampant. Business was paralyzed. Nothing was more certain and apparent than the disunity among the States.

Then came the great Constitutional Convention. The Convention was proposed, and carried through, in the living spirit of the Declaration of Independence. It presented to the world the unheard-of spectacle of a revolution without bloodshed.

The date was set for its convening, the 14th of May, 1787. However, a quorum of its delegates did not arrive in Philadelphia until the 25th, when the first, historic session opened in Constitution Hall. Seven States were represented. By month's end ten of the States were present and voting. The Maryland delegation arrived on June 2nd. Seven weeks later, on July 23rd, the delegates from New Hampshire arrived. As of July 10th, the New York delegation abstained from voting; and there was one absentee, Rhode Island, at that time hopelessly and helplessly in the hands of demagogues.

The twelve States had chosen as their delegates seventy-two of the leading men of the day. The largest number that ever was in attendance was fifty-five, and the number present when the Convention ended was thirty-nine. Benjamin Franklin was the oldest of the delegates, and one of the greatest men of his generation, or of any generation. George Washington was chosen unanimously to preside over the Convention's sessions, and few nations have any one man to whom they can ascribe the title of founder with as good reason as can the United States of America extend that title to George Washington. No nation has had a founder more truly great.

One of the younger men of the Convention to whom we are chiefly indebted for our knowledge of its proceedings was James Madison, a political scholar from Virginia. His faithfully kept and carefully preserved reports of the four months' toil in that Convention attest for all time the intelligent patriotism of the members. For six generations scholars have read those *Notes*, and always with awe and with respect.

Many of the delegates sent to Philadelphia were youngish men, but they were almost without exception educated and experienced—men of character, and substance, and social position. No group ever worked together more unselfishly or for a higher purpose than did the members of that Convention. There was among them no lusting for the limelight. One of their rules of order was absolute secrecy, and the respect that was given to that rule is hard for us to understand in this age of candid cameras, and newspapers, and radios, and television.

The work of the Convention was at no time easy. The problems that faced the delegates seemed insoluble, the difficulties appeared insurmountable. The Constitution itself was the result of magnificent, elastic compromise, of patient effort at agreement between the more radical and the more conservative delegates. The main question was: Should the new structure be a federal government, that is, a league of States; or should it be in truth a consolidated Union? From the first there was a conflict of opinion between the larger States and the smaller ones, chiefly on the matter of representation in the government: the large and powerful States naturally feeling that representation should be on the basis of population, or of taxable wealth, or both; the smaller States insisting that there should be equality of representation in the national Congress, they having exactly the same representation as the larger ones. The former theory rested upon the philosophy that a new nation was being born; the latter rested upon the belief that the separate States were sovereign and absolute, and that these sovereign States should have equal and similar representation in the national legislative body.

Some of the delegates argued that they were empowered to do nothing more than revise the Articles of Confederation; others insisted that their business was to write a constitution for a new nation.

The debating in the Convention was on high levels, generally characterized by personal self-effacement. Political principles rather than individual prejudices were, for the most part, given right of way. Once in a while debate became acrimonious, and once in a while threats of withdrawal were made. From the beginning it was apparent that a crisis would be reached concerning the representation of the States in the proposed national Congress. On July 16th the great compromise was achieved. Two houses of Congress were provided for: a House of Representatives, in which the States would have representation on the basis of population; and a Senate, in which each State would have equal representation, irrespective of its size or wealth.

Through arduous toil, and in a spirit of give and take, the Convention finally agreed upon the principles which would determine the Congress, the chief executive, and the judiciary. Then, on July 26th, they recessed until August 6th, and a Committee on Detail was instructed to whip these principles into practical shape during the ten-day interlude. The report of this Committee was the Constitution in embryo.

For a month following the 6th of August the Convention studied meticulously every phrase and every word of the draft submitted. Earnest debate ensued. The way those men comported themselves during that Convention fully justifies the appraisement which James Madison made:

> Whatever may be the judgment pronounced on the competency of the architects of the Constitution, or whatever

> may be the destiny of the edifice prepared by them, I feel it a duty to express my profound and solemn conviction, derived from my intimate opportunity of observing and appreciating the views of the Convention, collectively and individually, that there never was an assembly of men, charged with a great and arduous trust, who were more pure in their motives, or more exclusively or anxiously devoted to the object committed to them.

On September 8th the Convention appointed a Committee on Style. This Committee was composed of men who had demonstrated to their fellow members that they possessed unusual powers of comprehension and analysis, and a capacity for employing the English language with lucidity and conciseness of expression. The final literary style was probably that of Gouverneur Morris more than of any other. On September 15th the work of drafting was regarded as finished, and the Constitution was ordered engrossed for signing.

Concerning this immortal instrument of government, James Bryce, Viscount of Dechmont, has said:

> The Constitution of the United States, including the amendments, may be read aloud in twenty-three minutes. It is about half as long as Saint Paul's Epistle to the Corinthians, and one-fourth as long as the Irish Land Act of 1881. History knows few instruments which in so few words lay down equally momentous rules on a vast range of matters of the highest importance and complexity.

On September 17th the Convention met for the last time. Thirty-nine of the fifty-five who attended the Convention were present at the end. No one was enthusiastic over the result. Deep convictions had been yielded by everyone. Concessions had been made by all. The Constitution was so much the result of compromise that no member of the Convention felt pride of authorship in it. On the last day Benjamin Franklin pleaded for its support in one of the most cogent and pleasantly witty and impressive speeches of his notable career. In the course of this address he expressed a judgment which perhaps was typical of the convictions held by most of the members: that the Constitution was not perfect, but that it was the best that could be gotten, and if it should fail of adoption, the country would drift further and further into anarchy and chaos and bloodshed.

On this last day the great Washington addressed the delegates for the only time during the entire Convention: "Should the states reject this excellent Constitution," he said, "the probability is that an opportunity will never again offer to cancel another in peace—the next will be drawn in blood."

The proposed Constitution was sent to Congress, which was meeting in New York, in order that that body might formally consider its recommendation to the States for their adoption. The requirement was made that the Constitution must be adopted by Conventions in at least nine of the States before it could become effective.

The ratification of the Constitution was hotly debated and contested. Speaking by and large—and not too accurately—the uneducated and debtor class, the back-country folk and the small business people and farmers were opposed to it; and the educated and substantial people in business and the professions favored it. Nevertheless, some of the finest minds in America, and some of her most aristocratic leaders, too, were against it, and many of the humbler folk were for it. For a year and a half the great battle of political and philosophical forensics was waged. It seemed all but impossible to secure the Constitution's ratification by the required nine States. But before these eighteen months were gone, eleven of the thirteen States had ratified the Nation's fundamental law. Rhode Island and North Carolina ratified the Constitution after Washington's inauguration.

The framers of the Constitution stated its purposes in the Preamble, succinct, concise, comprehensive:

> We, the People of the United States, in Order to form a more perfect Union, establish Justice, insure domestic

Tranquility, provide for the common defence, promote the general Welfare, and secure the Blessings of Liberty to ourselves and our Posterity, do ordain and establish this Constitution for the United States of America.

"We, the People" had done this. With the founders of the Nation—and to every distant king and statesman—the fact and phrase were epochal.

The great fight was over. England, in signing the treaty which ended the Revolutionary War, would name each one of the thirteen States separately, but the people within them had now declared otherwise. A *Nation* had been created, and its Constitution had made those people one, under God, indivisible! The citizens of America had so ordained.

"We, the People, . . . do ordain and establish this Constitution . . ."

Here is no temporary expediency. No provision is made for secession of any State that voluntarily adopts it. This Union is to stand in perpetuity.

John Marshall, one of the greatest of all Chief Justices of the Supreme Court, stated the political philosophy of the Constitution when he declared that "The government of the United States has been emphatically termed a government of laws, and not of men." Yet the Constitution itself is not so much a code of laws as it is a charter granted by the people to a Federal government. That government was to be their protection against aggression from without and from injustice within. The Constitution is the norm or standard by which all laws must be tested. It points plainly to the *American* principle that just governments obtain their authority from the consent of the governed; that governments properly are the servants, and not the masters, of people. It lays down rules by which the government and its agencies may be controlled, and states that that control resides supremely in those who comprise its citizenry, the people.

It has been pointed out that there are four basic principles of the Constitution. The first is representative government. That is, legislation is not accomplished by the people directly, but by the chosen representatives of the people.

The second principle of the Constitution is the dual form of government which it establishes. Under it, the people of America are citizens of their respective States in matters which constitutionally are reserved to the States; at the same time they are citizens of the general government, and therefore cease to be citizens of the several States in those spheres of government which are delegated to the central and unifying power. Thus the people are constitutionally free to make their own laws in their various States, but those laws must not be out of harmony with the principles of the Constitution of the United States.

The third principle is the guaranty of individual liberty through constitutional limitations upon the powers of government itself.

The fourth principle is that of an independent judiciary. This unique principle is closely allied to the doctrine of limited governmental powers. The creation of an independent judiciary is really the balance wheel of the mechanism of the Constitution, and its supreme importance was not overstated by Justice William Wirt, of Maryland and Virginia: "If the Judiciary be struck from the system, what is there of any value that will remain; for government cannot subsist without it? It would be as rational to talk of a solar system without a sun."

The framers of the Constitution ransacked history for models, hints, suggestions, for help of any kind in the work which they were elected to accomplish. They found nowhere in history any instrument which they could copy. Only in the colonial meeting-house did they find encouragement, and there, as Calvin Coolidge would one day say, the Founding Fathers of the Republic discovered much of what they wanted. There was one thing, though, which their knowledge of history had taught them, and that was that in order to enjoy freedom under *any* form of government the powers of that government had to be balanced and divided, and that every person connected with the government must be effectively checked, and restrained by others.

In 1787, John Adams wrote: "If there is one certain truth to be collected from the history of all ages, it is this: That the people's rights and liberties, and the democratic mixture in a constitution, can never be preserved without a strong executive, or, in other words, without separating the executive power from the legislature." Thus the President's powers are checked by Congress, and those of Congress are checked by the President; and each one is held within the strict limitations of the Constitution by a Supreme Court, and the Court itself is checked by its own specifically defined jurisdictions, and by the Congress.

The Constitution makes provision for its own amendment. The method is difficult enough to make rash and reckless schemes run the gantlet of time and scrutiny, yet it is sufficiently easy of accomplishment that any provision which really needs amendment can have it without undue delay. Since our government was organized there have been more than two thousand amendments proposed, yet such has been the excellence of its founders' structure that the people in their wisdom have endorsed less than one percent of them.

The first ten amendments constitute our Bill of Rights. It was necessary for the proponents of the Constitution to promise the adoption of this Bill of Rights in order to secure the ratification of the Constitution itself. The purpose was to make yet more explicit the rights and immunities which the basic document contained.

The first article sets forth specifically certain fundamental freedoms: "Congress," it reads, "shall make no law respecting an establishment of religion, or prohibiting the free exercise thereof; or abridging the freedom of speech, or of the press; or the right of the people peaceably to assemble, and to petition the Government for a redress of grievances."

Thence the Bill of Rights goes on to list and to specify certain personal guarantees: ". . . the right of the people to keep and bear Arms, shall not be infringed. No Soldier shall, in time of peace be quartered in any house, without the consent of the Owner, nor in time of war, but in a manner to be prescribed by law. The right of the people to be secure in their persons, houses, papers, and effects, against unreasonable searches and seizures, shall not be violated, . . ."

The right of free men to impartial trial and justice is specified: "No person shall be held to answer for a capital, or other infamous crime, unless on a presentment or indictment of a Grand Jury, . . . nor be deprived of life, liberty, or property, without due process of law; nor shall private property be taken for public use, without just compensation. . . . the accused shall enjoy the right to a speedy and public trial, by an impartial jury . . . and no fact tried by a jury, shall be otherwise re-examined in any Court of the United States, than according to the rules of the common law. Excessive bail shall not be required, nor excessive fines imposed, nor cruel and unusual punishments inflicted."

The two final articles of our Bill of Rights take care to specify that in enumerating certain rights in the main body of the Constitution there is no denial or disparagement of others *retained by the people*, and make it clear that powers not specifically delegated to the national government are reserved to the States and to the people.

This Bill of Rights, a definite and integral part of our Constitution—our modern, American counterpart of the Ten Commandments—is one of our most precious possessions. In dictator countries the masses allow the radio and the press to become instruments of their own self-delusion. In dictator countries men and women are persecuted because of their religious faith. In dictator countries there is no such thing as free speech or freedom of assembly. Instead, there is intolerance, and bigotry, and persecution. The liberties set forth and protected by our Constitution should make us all fight for the preservation of free speech and freedom of worship; for wherever they are denied to one bloc of a country's population, they will sooner or later be denied to another. And one must be careful in this, too, for, as the great Frenchman, François Marie Arouet de Voltaire, has been paraphrased: "I disapprove of what you say, but I will defend to the death your right to say it."

John Milton, the English poet, gave expression to a sentiment that we sometimes seem not to prize, perhaps because of the very fact that it is guaranteed to us by our Constitution, and we have become accustomed to it. Said Milton, "Give me the liberty to know, to utter, and to argue freely, according to conscience—above all liberties."

The free speech provision of our Bill of Rights is the safety valve upon the engine of our representative democracy. Tie down the valve, and you invite an explosion that can demolish the whole engine. Experience and common sense dictate that we should keep in top-flight working condition the safety valve that gives opportunity for the blowing off of excess steam.

All who love the Constitution—who love it intelligently—will vow with Thomas Jefferson, writing from the White House to Dr. Benjamin Rush on September 23rd, 1800: "I have sworn upon the altar of God, eternal hostility against every form of tyranny over the mind of man."

The Constitution has endured because it is worthy to endure. Bess Streeter Aldrich, in her *Song of Years,* makes a prominent citizen say, "The American Constitution, like one of those wondrous rocking stones reared by the Druids, which the finger of a child might vibrate to its center, yet the might of an army could not move from its place—the Constitution is so nicely poised that it seems to sway with every breath of passion, yet so firmly based in the hearts and affections of the people that the wildest storms of treason and fanaticism break over it."

In the midst of the Convention, at the time of its greatest crisis, when it seemed as though the delegates were doomed to failure, Benjamin Franklin made one of the greatest speeches of his distinguished lifetime. He spoke of the apparent inability of the Convention members to solve the problems which were confronting them; he stated his faith in an overruling Providence and in the power of prayer; and then he said:

> I have lived, sir, a long time, and the longer I live, the more convincing proofs I see of this truth: That *God governs in the affairs of men.* And if a sparrow cannot fall to the ground without His notice, is it probable that an empire can rise without His aid?

> We have been assured, sir, in the sacred writings, that "except the Lord build the House they labor in vain that build it." I firmly believe this; and I also believe that without His concurring aid we shall succeed in this political building no better than the builders of Babel. We shall be divided by our little partial local interest; our projects will be confounded, and we ourselves shall become a reproach and byword down to future ages. And, what is worse, mankind may hereafter from this unfortunate instance, despair of establishing governments by human wisdom and leave it to chance, war, and conquest.
>
> I therefore beg leave to move that henceforth prayers imploring the assistance of Heaven, and its blessings on our deliberations, be held in this Assembly every morning before we proceed to business, and that one or more of the clergy of this city be requested to officiate in that service.

The records do not show conclusively what the Convention finally did with Franklin's motion. Madison, who reports it, would indicate that nothing was done about it; but a younger member, Jonathan Dayton of New Jersey, who also reported it, says it was acted on favorably by the Convention.

Yet regardless of what action the Convention took, one thing is certain: If we would ourselves prize our religious rights, we must use them!

At the end of the Convention in which the Constitution was agreed upon, George Washington said: "We have raised a standard to which the good and wise can repair; the event is in the hands of God."

Years later the French historian, François Guizot, asked James Russell Lowell: "How long will the American Republic endure?"

Lowell replied: "As long as the ideas of the men who founded it continue dominant."

The period which will close the appointment
tth which my fellow citizens have honoured me, being
t very distant, and the time actually arrived, at which
eir thoughts must be designating the citizen who is to
lminister the Executive Government of the United
ates during the ensuing term, it may conduce to a
ore distinct expression of the public voice, that I should
prize such of my fellow citizens as may retain their
rtiality towards me, that I am not to be num-
ered among those out of whom a choice is to be
ade.

I beg them to be assured that the Resolu-
n which dictates this intimation has not been
ken without the strictest regard to the relation
ich as a dutiful citizen I bear to my country; and
t in withdrawing that tender of my service, which
ence in my situation might imply, I am not influ-
-enced

Friends and Fellow Citizens

The quotation ~~which you [illegible]~~
~~find in this foregoing~~ address, was compos[ed]
and intended to have been published in [the]
year 1792; in time to have announced [to]
the Electors of the President & Vice President of the Unite[d]
States, the determination of the former previous to the 2d Election ~~which herein~~
~~therein expressed before the Electors [illegible]~~ ~~to that of~~
~~could have been~~
~~be made~~: but the solicitude of my confidential ~~a few~~ frien[ds]
~~who were apprised of my intention, and~~
~~in whose judgment I did very much rel[y]~~
~~(particularly in one who is in favour to th[e]~~
~~democrat*) that I would suspend my dete[r]~~
~~mination~~, added to the peculiar situatio[n]
of our foreign affairs at that epoch, ~~ind~~ in[duced]

ce

~~* Mr Madison~~

tion at that event throughout the U States show how unfounded have been the suspicions propagated among them of a policy in the General Government and in the Atlantic States inimical to their interests in regard to the Mississippi. They have seen two Treaties concluded, that with Great Britain and that with Spain which secure to them every thing they could desire with respect to our foreign relations, towards confirming their prosperity — Will they not henceforth rely for the preservation of these advantages on that Union by which they were procured? Will they not reject those advisers, if any there are, who would sever ~~render~~ them from ~~alien to~~ their Brethren and connect them with Aliens?

In controuling, fellow Citizens, as far as possible the spirit of party it is ~~essential~~ indispensable that you should cultivate towards ~~for~~ each other mutual good will, mutual forbearance, mutual candour — that you should not construe differences of opinion about the ~~best~~ means of advancing the public good ~~as~~ into infallible indications of enmity to the Government, enmity to liberty, want of Integrity and patriotism. Inferences of this kind are often as false as they are uncharitable and aspersing. I have before hinted the necessity of blending with ~~a~~ due watchfulness over the conduct of your public Agents a just confidence in them — This is a point of great moment to your safety. Calumny will never spare even those who are the most faithful and able, and if it find too ready credit with you, the consequence per with domestic factions, to practise the arts of seduction, to mislead public opinion, to influence or awe the public Councils! — Such an attachment of a small or weak, towards a great & powerful Nation, dooms the former to be the satellite of the latter. —

Against the insidious wiles of foreign influence, (I conjure you to believe me, fellow citizens) the jealousy of a free people ought to be constantly awake, since history and experience prove that foreign influence is one of the most baneful foes of Republican Government. — But that jealousy to be useful must be impartial; else it becomes the instrument of the very influence to be avoided, instead of a defence against it. — Excessive partiality for one foreign nation and excessive dislike of another cause those whom they actuate to see danger only on one side, and serve to veil and even second the arts of influence on the other. — Real Patriots, who may resist the intrigues of the favourite, are liable to become suspected and odious; while its tools and dupes usurp the applause & confidence of the people, to surrender their interests. —

The Great rule of conduct for us, in regard to foreign Nations is in extending our commercial relations to have with them as little political connection as possible. — So far as we have already formed engagements let them be fulfilled with

—The name of American, which belongs to you, in your national capacity, must always exalt the just pride of Patriotism, more than any appellation derived from local dis-

George Washington's Farewell Address

[4]

OUR MAJOR AMERICAN PROPHET is George Washington, and the greatest of his prophecies was his *Farewell Address*. In popular thought, a prophet is one who foretells, yet a more important function of the prophet is to *forth*tell, and forth-telling includes moral teaching—by warning, consoling, exhorting, and by giving examples of the things talked about. In that sense George Washington was a major prophet. His Farewell Address set the standards of American patriotism.

Washington was a man sent of God. He possessed all the essential qualities for the dynamic leadership required of one called to his exalted position. He was well born. He had a strong physique—tall, rugged, clear-eyed; a mighty man, with body and limbs of iron. He was a man of great dignity, carrying in his very presence that something which we call prestige. The training which he received as a soldier, added to his native abilities, made him one of the greatest military strategists of all time. His courage was sublime, covering the whole range of physical courage, military courage, and moral courage. He knew no fear. He saw the right instinctively, and chose it just as instinctively. He never turned from duty's path, no matter where that path might lead.

Weems' *Life of Washington,* and America's hero-worship of the man, has prompted certain persons in these later years to overwork the debunking of his history. But even when the debunkers have done their worst, George Washington stands before us a giant, our greatest American. His personal character was never once impeached, nor his reputation sullied. At the time of the Revolutionary War he was, with one possible exception, the richest man in America. He might have gone to England and been lionized and fêted. He had everything to lose, and nothing at all to gain, by espousing the uncertain cause of the harassed colonists. Yet he threw in his lot with his fellow Americans, without hesitation or reserve. He went through all the awful years of struggle as the Commander in Chief of the Army, without taking a single cent of pay, and a part of the time he paid the ragged American soldiers out of his own pocket. He longed for the comforts of his gracious Mount Vernon home, but during all the years of the Revolution he visited it only once, and that for no more than a few hours when on a military trip from the North to the South. When the War ended he repaired to his estate on the sloping banks of the Potomac. He loved the delights of country life—the growing of flowers, the designing of hedge-bordered paths, the planning of the rotation of crops, the fellowship with his neighbors, the encouragement of the work of the local church. He sought no honors. He was truly modest, in the finest sense. He had none of that mock humility which some affect and which is little more than inverted pride. Some of his compatriots believed it was best for the Country to establish a monarchy, and they tried to persuade Washington to become its king. He refused even to consider the proposal.

But when anarchy stalked the Land; when it became evident that the Colonies which had held together during the Revolution through fear of the Redcoats now transferred that fear to fear of each other; when it was easy to foresee that thirteen jarring nation-states were developing where formerly thirteen Colonies had been, then Washington answered the call of duty and went to Philadelphia where he was quietly, and unanimously, elected President of the Constitutional Convention. He attended every session of that

Convention, from the day it opened on May 25th, 1787, until it adjourned on September 17th.

He returned then to Mount Vernon and its autumn-tinted leaves, speaking modestly of having grown old in the service of his Country, and of his eyesight having grown dim in the passing years. Now he was back on the gentle banks of the Potomac—this virile, silent man—to dream, perchance, of Boston and of Trenton, of Valley Forge, Monmouth, and of the final scene at Yorktown. Then he heard his Country calling him to be its first President under the now-adopted Constitution. He entered that service, too, quietly, a gentleman of Virginia.

The first years were bound to be the most severely exacting, for they were the testing period of the revolutionary Constitution. Some critics of its provisions felt that the President had been given too much power; others felt that he had not been given enough. Too much power would end in tyranny, and too much liberty would end in its harbinger, anarchy. Moral balance was the supreme need of the infant Republic. Only with a President whose inner powers could deeply appreciate the value of each fine, delicate principle within that Constitution, and with the force to impel its recognition, could the Republic itself survive its infancy. Washington, with his tremendous understanding of principles and of men, was the man of destiny for that hour. He was President from April 30th, 1789, until March 4th, 1797.

Those eight years were filled with precedent-making responsibilities. It thrills one to read the history of Washington's administration and see how he, with the unerring instinct of a bird of flight, went straight to the heart of every problem, and found its solution in ways that stand the test of time, even to this hour.

Toward the end of his administration rival parties began to find fault and to criticize. Personal ambition and lust for political power or preferment, and sometimes conscientious political philosophy—like that of Thomas Jefferson—made Washington's heavy burden heavier still, and threw difficulties onto the steep road that he and the Nation then were climbing. Therefore, in the fall of 1796, as the day for the election of a new Chief Executive approached, Washington felt the time had come to tell his fellow countrymen that he would not stand for election to a third term. There is good reason to believe that it was Washington's conviction that it was better for the Country that one man should not hold power for too long a time. He decided upon the writing of what he called his Farewell Address.

For many years after it was published all sorts of charges of plagiarism were raised against the composition, it even being declared that the Address had been written by Alexander Hamilton. The storm has long since subsided, for historical research has revealed the facts. Washington was in the habit of seeking the assistance of his colleagues, constantly and intimately, in every matter he handled. When they were present with him he asked them for their counsel; when they were absent, he sought their advice by letter. It is a matter of common knowledge to historians that Washington asked and received help from his most trusted associates in the preparation of many of his great state papers. When he decided to compose a final message to his fellow countrymen he wrote a rough draft of what he had in mind and sent it to Alexander Hamilton, with the request that it be returned with any suggestions that his friend might have for its improvement. In reply, Hamilton sent the President an enlargement of the draft together with his observations. Washington took the comments and the addendum and studied them, recast them in his own words and sent them back to Hamilton. This sort of thing went on between the two for some time, and Hamilton's contribution throughout was that of a trusted friend and colleague. Finally, Washington was satisfied. His text, revised and then revised again, at last contained what he wanted to say and in the way he wanted to say it. He had expressed his American philosophy, and his conclusions in its regard.

What are those conclusions? It is as though the Address were the last will and testament of the Father of his Country, to his Country. It is a bequest of devotion, and advice.

A single exhortation of Washington's has been so oft quoted, and so bandied about by men in and out of politics that many of us are apt to think that the whole of Washington's Farewell Address was a warning against entangling alliances. There is warning, yes; but it is one which must be taken within its context.

As a matter of fact, an "isolationist" can badly err in his use of the Farewell Address. What did Washington say?

> Observe good faith & justice towards all Nations. Cultivate peace and harmony with all—Religion & morality enjoin this conduct; and can it be that good policy does not equally enjoin it?—It will be worthy of a free, enlightened, and, at no distant period, a great Nation, to give to mankind the magnanimous and too novel example of a People always guided by an exalted justice & benevolence. . . .
>
> In the execution of such a plan nothing is more essential than that permanent, inveterate antipathies against particular Nations and passionate attachment for others should be excluded;—and that in place of them just & amicable feelings towards all should be cultivated.

That is the context in which his advice not to "entangle our peace and prosperity in the toils of European Ambition, Rivalship, Interest, Humour or Caprice" must be taken, and understood. And in this context Washington pointed out the dangers inherent in "permanent alliances, with any portion of the foreign world"—in order that we might be free to "choose peace or War, as our interest guided by justice shall counsel."

Washington was no isolationist. He sent commissioners abroad to negotiate treaties of commerce. He advised faithful performance of treaties made. His "predominant motive", he said, was "to endeavour to gain time to our country to settle & mature its yet recent institutions". And in this he succeeded, magnificently. He did not advise aloofness; he counseled harmony. "Harmony, liberal intercourse with all Nations", were his urgency, as each was "recommended by policy, humanity and interest." The relationships against which Washington truly counseled were the "Excessive partiality for one foreign nation and excessive dislike of another". He warned against a sycophantic and servile attitude toward any nation, and at the same time he warned equally against baiting and irritating any. He pleaded that in our commercial policy we not grant "exclusive favours or preferences" but that we hold out "an equal and impartial hand" to all.

This advice concerning our relationship with foreign countries was but one item in Washington's great, prophetic utterance.

He pleaded as did the "angels, trumpet-tongued against The deep damnation" of disunion. The structure of government which made of the people of all the American States one Nation, indivisible, was, he insisted, a gigantic pillar in the edifice of our true independence. He argued cogently against anything that might mar the essential unity which the Constitution of the United States had created. He urged Americans to accustom themselves to think and speak of the Constitution as the palladium of their political prosperity and safety. He therefore warned against whatever might make for disunion; against geographical discriminations and sectional jealousies; against disrespect for the legitimate authority of the Union; against obstructions to the execution of the laws enacted pursuant to its Constitution; against lawlessness of every kind. Speaking of the government, he said: "Respect for its authority, compliance with its Laws, acquiescence in its measures, are duties enjoined by the fundamental maxims of true Liberty. . . . The very idea of the power and the right of the People to establish Government presupposes the duty of every individual to obey the established Government."

He counseled against a spirit of innovation which would alter, and thus impair, the energy of the great federal system. He argued for a vigorous protection of those provisions of the Constitution which distribute, adjust and limit the delegated powers of government itself. He exhorted against selfish partisanship, pointing out that "The alternate domination of one faction over another, sharpened by the spirit of revenge . . . . is itself a frightful despotism" and his words have made it forever plain that when men grow tired of the "disorders & miseries, which result," and seek to find security and repose in the absolute power of some one individual, "sooner or later the chief of some prevailing faction more able or more fortunate than his competitors, turns this disposition to the purposes of his own elevation, on the ruins of Public Liberty."

Again he declares that the members of the government—the President, the members of the Congress, and all the others—should confine their activities to those spheres which are permitted by the Constitution, not allowing the powers of one department to encroach upon another. "The spirit of encroachment", he forewarns, "tends to consolidate the powers of all the departments in one, and thus to create whatever the form of government, a real despotism." If there be discovered something wrong in the distribution of constitutional powers, "let it be corrected by an amendment in the way which the Constitution designates.—But let there be no change by usurpation. . . ."

Further along in his Address Washington expressed his principles with regard to fiscal responsibility. His opening sentence was a summation: "As a very important source of strength & security, cherish public credit." This was of the utmost importance, he felt, and he advised that in time of peace we should not add to our public debts but should then "discharge the Debts which unavoidable wars may have occasioned, not ungenerously throwing upon posterity the burthen which we ourselves ought to bear."

In this prophetic utterance the Father of our Country noted well that "virtue or morality is a necessary spring of popular government", and he admonished, therefore, that "Institutions for the general diffusion of knowledge" be promoted. This wish was very personal to him, and in his will he not only bequeathed money to one such institution but set aside further money toward the establishment of a national university. He acted, as always, upon the counsel which he gave to others, and nothing in his Address was more emphatically set forth than this: "Promote then as an object of primary importance, Institutions for the general diffusion of knowledge.—In proportion as the structure of a government gives force to public opinion, it is essential that public opinion should be enlightened."

Washington referred to the admonitions of his Address as "these counsels of an old and affectionate friend". He did not often speak of things as "indispensable", but now he permitted himself to do so. He said: "Of all the dispositions and habits which lead to political prosperity, Religion and morality are indispensable supports." He impeached the very patriotism of one "who should labour to subvert these great Pillars of human happiness, these firmest props of the duties of Men & citizens." Neither property, nor reputation, nor life is secure, he said, when people fail to be religious, fully and sincerely. And in this emphasis George Washington's life squared wholly with his words. He was a deeply religious man, and was unshakable in his faith in the life hereafter. He believed in the efficacy of prayer, and in the overruling providence of Almighty God. He lived his faith, and the faith he held shone through his Farewell Address strong and steady, as a beacon.

Such is the prophecy of George Washington. His life and being were dependent upon no praise, nor were they disturbed by fame. He did not think more highly of himself than was modestly proper. He met the duties of the day with a resolute serenity. Men—the Duke of Wellington, for instance—pronounced him "the purest and noblest character of modern times", and Abraham Lincoln said of him: "Washington is the mightiest name of earth—long since mightiest in the cause of civil liberty; still mightiest in moral reformation. On that name no eulogy is expected."

His religious faith was the source and inspiration of his noble life.

O say, can you see, ~~through~~ by the dawn's early light,
What so proudly we hail'd at the twilight's last gleaming,
Whose broad stripes & bright stars through the perilous fight
O'er the ramparts we watch'd, were so gallantly streaming?
And the rocket's red glare, the bomb bursting in air,
Gave proof through the night that our flag was still there,
O say does that star-spangled banner yet wave
O'er the land of the free & the home of the brave?

On the shore dimly seen through the mists of the deep,
Where the foe's haughty host in dread silence reposes,
What is that which the breeze, o'er the towering steep,
As it fitfully blows, half conceals, half discloses?
Now it catches the gleam of the morning's first beam,
In full glory reflected now shines in the stream,
'Tis the star-spangled banner — O long may it wave
O'er the land of the free & the home of the brave!

And where is that band who so vauntingly swore,
That the havoc of war & the battle's confusion
A home & a Country should leave us no more?
— ~~[illegible]~~
Their blood has wash'd out their foul footstep's pollution.
No refuge could save the hireling & slave
From the terror of flight or the gloom of the grave,
And the star-spangled banner in triumph doth wave
O'er the land of the free & the home of the brave.

O thus be it ever when freemen shall stand
Between their lov'd home & the war's desolation!
Blest with vict'ry & peace may the heav'n rescued land
Praise the power that hath made & preserv'd us a nation!
Then conquer we must, when our cause it is just,
And this be our motto — "In God is our trust,"
And the star-spangled banner in triumph shall wave
O'er the land of the free & the home of the brave. —

THE

STAR SPANGLED BANNER

A PARIOTIC SONG.

2

the shore dimly seen through the mists of the deep,
here the foe's haughty host in dread silence reposes,
t is that which the breeze, o'er the towering steep,
s it fitfully blows, half conceals, half discloses;
it catches the gleam of the morning's first beam,
ll glory reflected new shines in the stream,
'Tis the star spangled banner, O, long may it wave
O'er the land of the free, and the home of the brave.

(3)

And where is that band who so vauntingly swore
That the havoc of war and the battle's confusion,
A home and a country, shall leave us no more,
Their blood has wash'd out their foul footsteps pollution.
No refuge could save the hireling and slave,
From the terror of flight or the gloom of the grave,
And the star spangled banner, in triumph doth wave,
O'er the Land &c.

(4)

O! thus be it ever when freemen shall stand,
Between their lov'd home, and the war's desolation,
Blest with vict'ry and peace, may the Heav'n rescued land,
Praise the Pow'r that hath made and preserv'd us a nation!
Then conquer we must, when our cause it is just,
And this be our motto—"In God is our Trust";
And the star spangled banner, in triumph shall wave,
O'er the Land &c.

Blest with vict'ry & peace may the heav'n rescued land
Praise the power that hath made & preserv'd us a nation!

"The Star-Spangled Banner"

[4]

NATIONAL SONGS are born of patriotism. The song of Deborah, the psalm of Moses and many of the psalms of David, reveal a passionate patriotism. The same principle holds true for every people and in every age.

The soldiers of the Revolution marched to the tune of *Yankee Doodle*, and the thin, shrill calls of fifes and the staccato roll of drums were heard from Fort Moultrie down in Carolina to the forests of Vermont. In succeeding generations we find Americans singing *Hail, Columbia*; *America*; *The Battle Hymn of the Republic*; *Dixie*; and many, many others.

The one song whose patriotic mood, for a century and a half, has claimed the hearts of our people is *The Star-Spangled Banner*. It must be included in the roots of true Americanism.

"If I may write the songs of a people", said Andrew Fletcher of Saltoun, "I care not who writes its laws." What this Scottish publicist of three centuries ago meant to convey was that the behavior of a people is as much determined by sentiment as it is by legislation. As an eagle rises on its wings, so society is borne onward and upward by reason and affection, equally.

It was Shelley who wrote that "Poets are the hierophants of unapprehended inspiration; the mirrors of the gigantic shadows which futurity casts upon the present." Those who have the spirit of song within them are all one clan, be they harpers among the herdsmen, musicians at the courts of kings, or minstrels or troubadours, ballad peddlers or poets laureate. They are a tribe, and to them is bequested the honor and glory of recording and preserving whatever is fine and worthwhile in the spirit of the times. Francis Scott Key was one of them.

He was a lawyer, a young man of thirty-three who had once aspired to the ministry, and whose gentle nature often expressed itself in verse. The critics say that he was no poet. I do not know that anybody will argue with them about this, so let us readily concede that as a poet he was a very modest one.

But it has happened more than once that a man who was not a major poet has written some one great piece of poetry, as was the case with Josef Mohr, a parish priest in the countryside near Salzburg. Father Mohr was attending a meeting in the little schoolhouse at Arnsdorf, on the Christmas Eve of 1818, when he asked to be excused to make some notes. A few minutes later he returned, and handed a single sheet of paper to his friend Franz Gruber, the village schoolmaster. Gruber was an organist, too, and as he read the words his priestly friend had written he seemed to hear a music in the background, and thus a song was born. In the valleys and the mountains of the Tyrol, the choristers of a hundred hamlets began to sing it, and it went out over Austria, over Germany, to enter into the hearts of untold generations. It came to be the hallmark, as it were, of the immortal Ernestine Schumann-Heink—she who named her youngest son George Washington. A village priest and a young country schoolmaster gave it to the world, on Christmas Eve a century and a half ago, and enriched its treasury with their belovèd *Silent Night, Holy Night.*

What two young men of Austria gave to the world in 1818 Francis Scott Key gave uniquely to America. On August 27th, 1814, a physician, Dr. William Beanes, had been taken out of his bed in the middle of the night by a company of His Majesty's marines and confined to the brig of a British man-of-war. One of the doctor's closest friends, Francis Scott Key, of Frederick, Maryland, was serving in the Georgetown field artillery. Through the influence of Chief Justice Taney of the United States Supreme Court, Key secured permission from President Madison to visit the enemy fleet, then lying to in Chesapeake Bay, and under a flag of truce to obtain the release of Dr. Beanes if possible. Accompanied by another lawyer, John S. Skinner, who was governmental agent for the exchange of prisoners, Key took a small dispatch boat on September 7th and made directly for the British flagship *Tonnant.* Their reception was hostile, until letters—which Key thoughtfully had obtained from a number of British wounded—were handed to Vice Admiral Cochrane and the enemy commander read the words of appreciation for the treatment that British soldiers were receiving in the hospitals of the Americans.

Dr. Beanes was given into the custody of the two men, but the three were informed they could not be released until the pending move on Baltimore had taken place. On the 10th *Tonnant* sailed toward the Patapsco River in preparation for the attack. The waters proved to be too shallow for the ship, and the three were transferred to the frigate *Surprise,* commanded by Thomas Cochrane, son of the admiral. *Tonnant* was sent into deeper waters and the admiral raised his flag to the topmast of *Surprise.* The three Americans were now put on their dispatch boat and she was ordered to anchor behind the ships-of-the-line in preparation for the coming action. It commenced by land on the morning of the 13th, and in the late afternoon by sea.

The day wore on, anxiously. As evening fell, the guns of Fort McHenry were still replying, and the British bombardment continued without abatement. The Americans witnessed the entire action from their anchorage, and Key told about it afterward. Each time a shell was fired, he said, they would watch it in its trajectory, and each time Dr. Beanes, whose eyesight was extremely poor, would pluck his sleeve and ask him: "What do you see?" They watched for the Fort's return fire, counting the minutes fearfully, for they knew that only so long as McHenry's guns replied the Fort had not surrendered. All that night, by "the rocket's red glare, the bombs bursting in air", they could see that the American Flag was still waving over the ramparts on the shore. The huge Flag, stitched by Mrs. Mary Young Pickersgill, widow, bore the red and white horizontal stripes of the fifteen States, and measured 42 by 30 feet.

A short time before dawn the firing ceased, and with the

sudden closing down of darkness came a time of awful tension and suspense. Key did not know but that the Fort had been taken; he did know, though, that if the guns of McHenry had been silenced it meant the surrender and razing of Baltimore. Then came "the dawn's early light", and as Key gazed shoreward toward the flag-staff above Fort McHenry he saw where a great, gaping hole had been made by a bombshell passing directly through the banner, and that its edges were in tatters where another shell had exploded nearby. But he saw "that our flag was still there", and at that instant the song came to him. He jotted down on the back of a letter the words and phrases and lines as they raced through his mind, and as the British ships of war withdrew he kept on, sitting in the little boat as it was rowed to shore. At the Fountain Inn on Light Street, near Orange Alley, he enlarged upon what he had written, smoothed it, and completed the words as they stand today. He used the meter of a song that was popular at the time, and set them to its tune, *Anacreon in Heaven.*

In the morning he took his composition to his brother-in-law, Judge Joseph Nicholson, captain of a volunteer company which had served the day before. The Judge liked it, and suggested that it be called *The Defense of Fort McHenry.* They took it to the shop of the *Baltimore American* where Samuel Sands, a 14-year-old printer's devil, set it to type and struck off copies in the form of handbills. That evening, in the old McConkey Tavern next to the Holliday Street Theater, Captain Edes of the volunteer Pennsylvania militia, down from York, read the words to his recruits. One of them, an 18-year old actor named Ferdinand Durang, glanced through the music quickly, mounted an old rush-bottomed chair, and began to sing. The tavern was an instant, joyous bedlam. Four months later the song of Francis Scott Key was given its present title.

For more than a century we sang it, along with *America,* and *Hail, Columbia,* and *Marching Through Georgia,* on our patriotic occasions, and then a bill was introduced in Congress to declare it our official Anthem. The bill, introduced on January 30th, 1913, was referred to the Committee on the Judiciary. It died in committee.

The first official recognition of *The Star-Spangled Banner* came in 1916 when President Woodrow Wilson designated it for all state occasions in answer to a departmental demand that a single piece of music be named as standard. That gave it a place during and after the first world war that was not accorded to any other American air. Then, on March 3rd, 1931, one hundred and seventeen years after its composition, the United States Congress passed the bill that made *The Star-Spangled Banner* our National Anthem.

No other writing in the collection which I feel best expresses the roots of true Americanism has had to stand up against such criticism as has this, our Nation's Anthem. It is perennially attacked. Some say that the tune is unsingable; more often, however, the criticism comes from persons who honestly feel that it is not expressive of the American spirit at its best. Some attack it because they seem to feel that it fosters a different spirit, one of militarism and of narrow nationalism. Let us examine it in the light of such viewpoints.

Nationalism may be either a good thing or a bad thing, of course. Nationalism that is aggressive and bellicose, is to be condemned. It results both from feelings of superiority and from feelings, oddly enough, of inferiority. Those afflicted with the former strut because they see themselves as victors; and the latter feel impelled to bluster because they sense somehow that they have been vanquished. Nationalism that is selfish, and self-centered, and wrapped in the cloak of a narrow self-interest, is in the light of all history self-defeating. Nationalism that rides rough-shod over the rights of weaker nations, that menacingly carries the "big stick", that struts and blusters and dares others to challenge it; that arrogantly takes by force and violence what it wants from near or distant neighbors—such nationalism menaces, and always has menaced, the peace of the world, and is bad and only bad. Nationalism, often called patriotism, that makes a fetish of the symbols of government, and that prates the adolescent sophistry that his country is always right, and never wrong—that kind of nationalism is what Samuel Johnson had in mind when he declared it "the last refuge of a scoundrel." It is a form of tyranny, too, albeit somewhat self-imposed.

But, rightly understood, nationalism—patriotism—is one of the noblest of man's sentiments, and one of the most sovereign instincts of a good man. The absence of it indicates a dead soul, as Sir Walter Scott once wrote, in his *Lay of the Last Minstrel*:

> Breathes there the man, with soul so dead,
> Who never to himself hath said,
> This is my own, my native land!

To this there may be added the patriotism of the prophets of ancient Israel. Patriotism meant to them more than an emotional thrill. They had the sentiment; their longing for Jerusalem when they were exiled; and their joy at the sight of the Holy City, as set forth in the Psalms, bear witness to the fervency of their affection for their country. But their patriotism was also shot through with an ethical passion. They proved their patriotism by denouncing the sins which like dry rot ate out the very life and substance of their nation.

There is nothing in *The Star-Spangled Banner* which properly can be interpreted as expressive of a narrow nationalism as against the higher patriotism of world brotherhood. On Commonwealth Avenue in Boston there is an impressive statue of William Lloyd Garrison, inscribed with one of his immortal utterances: "My country is the world; my countrymen are mankind." That is Christian patriotism. It takes the spirit of Christ's Sermon on the Mount and makes it the Magna Carta of our Nation; and it invokes the spirit of the good Samaritan as the guiding principle of our conduct, in the neighborhood of nations.

That which is vital and intelligent in patriotism comes not from an exclusive love of one's own country, but from self-forgetfulness in a dedication to the larger idea of humanity. If the triumph of patriotism means the discomfiture of other nations, or the quenching of their legitimate aspirations, then patriotism is tyranny under a pleasant name.

Unless a man loves something higher than national conceit and material advantage, he can love his country neither wisely nor worthily. The true patriot loves his country as he loves himself;

that is, he loves truth and justice, and he loves honor, seeking these for himself and for his nation. True patriotism is a moral thing, for "Righteousness exalteth a nation: but sin is a reproach to any people."

The patriotism of a mature mind requires us to raise a race of patriots who are ready to die for their Country, and this is meet, and right. But the man who makes his country *worth* dying for is a man worthy of no lesser honor.

America must be an example of international cooperation and good will. We must allow no spirit of national greed and selfishness to find rootage in the soil of this great continent. For it was in this spirit that our first American President bade us his farewell—

> —that your union & brotherly affection may be perpetual—that the free constitution, which is the work of your hands, may be sacredly maintained—that its administration in every department may be stamped with wisdom and virtue—that, in fine, the happiness of the people of these States, under the auspices of liberty, may be made complete, by so careful a preservation and by so prudent a use of this blessing as will acquire to them the glory of recommending it to the applause, the affection—and adoption of every nation which is yet a stranger to it.

With such thoughts in mind, let us look at *The Star-Spangled Banner* and see if the harsh things that so frequently are said about it are indeed not unworthy of its grace and meaning.

It is full of the imagery of battle, of course, yet it is not the battle that is glorified, it is the Flag. Nowhere in the song is there a glorification of war for war's own sake, or of war as a national policy for the Nation's aggrandizement. The person who sees only the "rocket's red glare", and "the bombs bursting in air", and "the foe's haughty host" has missed the whole point of the Anthem. The feeling that surges through its entire composition is born of the sight of the Flag! It is the banner, the *symbol,* that is loved, not war.

It may not be out of place to observe that the Flag of the

United States is a *beautiful* thing. Nor is this judgment necessarily inspired by one's sentimental regard for the Nation which it represents. From a purely aesthetic point of view its design, its geometrical proportions, and the arrangement of its colors constitute it the most beautiful national banner in the world. Of course it was once no more than a piece of bunting or silk that lay upon the floor of a warehouse. But when it becomes the Flag, it is the symbol of the American's being and government. One does not need to pass from the thing signified to the symbol of its significance and become an idolater of the latter to feel this swift response to the beauty of the Nation's emblem.

The Flag came into existence not quite a year after the Declaration of Independence. It was on June 14th, 1777, that the Continental Congress voted that the Flag of the United States of America should consist of thirteen red and white stripes, and a union of blue with thirteen stars. For a while a stripe and a star were added for each new State admitted to the Union. But before long Congress ordained that the Flag should consist of the thirteen original stripes of alternate red and white, and that in the little square heaven of blue there should be one star for each of the States within the Union. Thus the Flag has thirteen stripes, and in its heaven now shine fifty stars—the most glorious constellation in all the firmament of nations.

There is a philosophy of colors. The particular shade of red in our Star-Spangled Banner is scarlet. It is a bright, brilliant red, orange-tinged. Thus the red of love and courage and passion, plus the blend of orange which stands for benevolence, give us the scarlet of the Feast of Martyrs—and of the Star-Spangled Banner. Red represents blood, and blood represents fire, and blood and fire are life, in the philosophy of colors.

White is the harmonious blending of all the hues and colors and beauties of light. White without any admixture of darkness sets forth the pure, absolute triumph of light. The writer of the Apocalypse tells us that the redeemed are arrayed in white robes, and then, as though he feared we might not grasp his symbolism, he hastens on to say that the white robes are the righteous acts of saints. It is no fictitious righteousness. It is the result of work and sacrifice, for we are told that the saints themselves "have washed their robes and made them white in the blood of the Lamb."

Thus American patriotism, as symbolized in our national emblem, aims at character that not only is spotless but also is complete—the combination of all virtues, the balancing of all excellences, a display of all the beauties of grace.

The white stars are set in a field of blue. Since blue is the color of the zenith of the clearest sky, it early came to be associated with heaven, and therefore was regarded as sacred. Blue is the color that traditionally symbolizes virtue. Virtue is integrity of character; it is moral behavior; it is conformity to the standards of right. It is honesty that goes beyond the mere requirements of "legal" honesty. Hence the blue in our Flag may be made to stand for that quality of pure patriotism that characterized the signers of the Declaration of Independence, and the framers of the Constitution of the Republic.

Stars stand not only for the States of the Union; they stand for ideals and aspirations—the aspirations of a free people, and the ideals of our citizenry, and their Nation. Our Flag is a constant summons to all Americans that they follow the star, ever onward, toward perfection, even as the wise men of old followed the Star that led them to a manger in silent Bethlehem.

Our national Anthem, *The Star-Spangled Banner,* glorifies the Flag not only because its stripes are stroked in ripples of white and red, and not only because its white stars laugh down their delightful light from the little square heaven of blue, but because the Flag is the symbol of the rights claimed for us by the Declaration of Independence and then reserved to us by the Constitution of the United States; because it is a pledge of liberty and justice, a promise that the rights of the weakest will be respected, wherever one sees the Flag against the sky.

Note particularly the final stanza of our national Anthem, and see how strikingly in harmony it is with the main drift of the roots of true Americanism:

Oh! thus be it ever, when freemen shall stand
Between their loved homes and the war's desolation!
Blest with victory and peace, may the heav'n rescued land
Praise the Power that hath made and preserved us a nation.
Then conquer we must, when our cause it is just,
And this be our motto: "In God is our trust."
And the star-spangled banner in triumph shall wave
O'er the land of the free and the home of the brave!

The spirit of our national Anthem is at one with the spirit of our forebears' Declaration of Independence. It was conceived in the same philosophy and teachings. And what were those teachings? President Calvin Coolidge, in an address in Philadelphia at the celebration of the one hundred and fiftieth anniversary of the signing of the Declaration, pronounced the inescapable, the "conclusion that in its great outlines the Declaration of Independence was the result of the religious teachings of the preceding period." He had made extended research, one which clearly showed him that the intellectual life of our forefathers "centered around the meetinghouse. They were intent upon religious worship. . . . They were a people who came under the influence of a great spiritual development and acquired a great moral power. No other theory is adequate to explain or comprehend the Declaration of Independence. It is the product of the spiritual insight of the people. . . . The things of the spirit come first. . . . We must follow the spiritual and moral leadership which they showed."

So spoke Calvin Coolidge, and that is the contention and the exhortation of *The Star-Spangled Banner.*

We can conquer only "when our cause it is just". We will be secure in our national safety only so long as we practice our Nation's motto: "In God is our Trust."

At this second appearing to take the oath of the presidential office, there is less occasion for an extended address than there was at the first. Then a statement, somewhat in detail, of a course to be pursued, seemed fitting and proper. Now at the expiration of four years, during which public declarations have been constantly called forth on every point and phase of the great contest which still absorbs the attention, and engrosses the energies of the nation little that is new could be presented. The progress of our arms, upon which all else chiefly depends, is as well known to the public as to myself; and it is, I trust, reasonably satisfactory and encouraging to all. With high hope for the future, no prediction in regard to it is ventured.

On the occasion corresponding to this four years ago, all thoughts were anxiously directed to an impending civil-war. All dreaded it— all sought to avert it. While the inaugeral address was being delivered from this place, devoted altogether to *saving* the Union without war, insurgent agents were in the city seeking to destroy it without war—seeking to dissolve the Union, and divide effects, by negotiation. Both parties deprecated war; but one of them would *make* war rather than let the nation survive; and the other would *accept* war rather than let it perish. And the war came.

One eighth of the whole population were colored slaves, not distributed generally over the Union, but localized in the Southern ~~half~~ part of it. These slaves constituted a peculiar and powerful interest. All knew that this interest was, somehow, the cause of the war. To strengthen, perpetuate, and extend this interest was the object for which the insurgents would rend the Union, even by war; while the government claimed no right to do more than to restrict the territorial enlargement of it. Neither party expected for the war, the magnitude, or the duration, which it has already attained. Neither anticipated that the *cause* of the conflict might cease with, or even before, the conflict itself should cease. Each looked for an easier triumph, and a result less fundamental and astounding. Both read the same Bible, and pray to the same God; and each invokes His aid against the other. It may seem strange that any men should dare to ask a just God's assistance in wringing their bread from the sweat of other men's faces; but let us judge not that we be not judged. The prayers of both could not be answered; that of neither has been answered fully. The Almighty has His own purposes. "Woe unto the world because of offences! for it must needs be that offences come; but woe to that man by whom the offence cometh!" If we shall suppose that American Slavery is one of those offences which, in the providence of God, must needs come, but which, having continued through His appointed time, He now wills to remove, and that He gives to both North and South, this terrible war, as the woe due to those

by whom the offence came, shall we discern therein any departure from those divine attributes
which the believers in a Living God always
ascribe to Him? Fondly do we hope—fervently do we pray—that this mighty scourge of
war may speedily pass away. Yet, if God
wills that it continue, until all the wealth
piled by the bond-man's two hundred and
fifty years of unrequited toil shall be sunk,
and until every drop of blood drawn with the
lash, shall be paid by another drawn with
the sword, as was said three thousand years
ago, so still it must be said "the judgments
of the Lord, are true and righteous altogether"

With malice toward none;
with charity for all; with firmness in the
right, as God gives us to see the right,
let us strive on to finish the work we
are in; to bind up the nation's wounds;
to care for him who shall have borne the battle and for his widow, and his orphan—
to do all which may achieve and cherish a just,
and a lasting peace, among ourselves, and with ~~the world~~ all nations.

With malice toward none;
with charity for all; with firmness in the
right, as God gives us to see the right,

Abraham Lincoln's Second Inaugural Address

[6]

THE GOSPEL of Americanism *par excellence* is Abraham Lincoln's Second Inaugural Address. By every measurement, it is good news, glad tidings. It was spoken by the man who more than any other merits the appellation, "Saviour of the American Union."

Slavery was a vexatious question from the beginning of our national history until it came to its climax in the shock of Civil War. Some of the most eloquent passages in the Declaration of Independence, as originally it was drafted by Thomas Jefferson, inveighed against the enslavement of the negro people. Jefferson writhed as he saw the Continental Congress, under the lash of some of the delegations, cut those passages out of the final draft. The question came again to the front in the Constitutional Convention, and it was a live issue—to increase in its bitterness of feeling and peril for the ultimate safety of the Union—down to the days of tragedy that followed upon the firing on Fort Sumter.

Thanks partly to his superb abilities, partly to the trust which his fellow men had in him, and certainly to the overwhelming providence of God, Abraham Lincoln became the instrument for striking the shackles off the wrists and ankles of the slaves. Lincoln's arguments were based almost exclusively upon the philosophy which he absorbed from two documents: One was the New Testament, and the other was the Declaration of Independence. All of his *political* philosophy, he declared, could be traced to the Declaration. It was his application of the principles set forth in that immortal instrument that made him the trusted champion of the movement to save the Union and free the slaves.

How could a man like Lincoln, lacking even the meanest of the advantages, growing from his humble birth into full manhood an utter stranger to formal education, and with no "opportunity" whatsoever—how could such a man rise to the wonderful eminence which came to him? It is a long reach, indeed, from the rude cabin of an illiterate backwoodsman in Kentucky to the White House, the residence of Presidents. It is a long reach from the boy who lay upon the puncheon floor of a frontier home, grasping in his hands the books he studied by the flickering light of a burning pine knot, to the man who wrote the Gettysburg Address and the Second Inaugural. If ever Browning's dictum that "a man's reach should exceed his grasp" was applicable, it was applicable to Abraham Lincoln. He had an exceeding reach. Yet he had "no form nor comeliness", and in him there was "no beauty that we should desire him". But his soul was beautiful. He was lean and lank and tall, yet even his tall frame was not knee-high to his mind. His hands and feet were large and ungainly, but they were Lilliputian by comparison with his heart. His deep-set eyes became dark-circled and cavernous with brooding upon the sorrows of his belovèd Country.

His father did not amount to much in himself, but he was the sire of Abraham Lincoln, a sufficient glory for any man. His mother died when he was a lad of nine, and the heartbroken boy took sad and solitary journeys to her lonely forest grave. And beckoned gently by the memories of her example and teachings he found his haven in the far land of a noble life, and made it his.

As a boy he had only a half-dozen books to his name: *Robinson Crusoe, The Life of Washington, History of the United States,*

Aesop's Fables, *Pilgrim's Progress*, and the Holy Bible. But in his manhood, when a menaced Ship of State creaked and groaned in the stressful storms of war, his very strength made him as little understood by his fellows as was Robinson Crusoe by his man Friday on his far-off isle. His life in its noble traits even outshone those in Weems' great *Life of Washington* which he had so assiduously studied. He became at once the type and flower of the United States whose history he had absorbed, and he made more history than any other man of his day, anywhere. He rivaled Aesop in the fables which he told, setting all the countryside laughing at his homely yarns, even when a tempest of never-ending pain raged within his heart. He translated the Bible into a version the frontier people easily understood; he transmuted the words of the Holy Book into life and character. His whole career was a pilgrim's progress; he floundered through many a Slough of Despond; he struggled up the steep Hill Difficulty; he faced lions on the way. He fought his progress through the Valley of Humiliation and the Valley of the Death, but he reached the Delectable Mountains of service well done. And when he came finally to the River of Death, Mr. Good Conscience was there to ferry him across, to take his place in the Beulah Land of Immortal Renown.

As a youth he helped backwoodsmen at the "raisings", laboring with them to put up the rude log cabins where the settlers lived; as a man he held secure the ridge-pole of the House of State when a people, torn by hate and internecine strife, threatened its destruction. In his youth he did not hesitate to lift a pig out of the mire where it was stuck; as a man he lifted up a race that wallowed in the slough of slavery, and builded for it a temple of human freedom. As a youth he trounced the rowdies of the backwoods who would steal from the store he kept; as a man he subdued the rowdies of the Nation who fain would remove a single star from the Flag of the Union he so loved. As a child he learned his mother's will, and did it in such a way as to earn her hardy encomia; as a man he learned the direction in which his God was going, and then, with all his splendid strength, moved obstacles out of the way for His onward march.

The two greatest literary works that came out of the period of the Civil War were Lincoln's Gettysburg Address and the Second Inaugural. And of these, the Second Inaugural seems to me the greater. It is brief. Lincoln remarked in his first sentence that there was no occasion "for an extended address". Four years of terrible war, and the then recent course of events in that war, tell their own heartrending story.

The Second Inaugural was delivered at noon on March 4th, 1865, from the East Portico of the Capitol. It had been raining earlier in the morning, and the whole forenoon was dark with scudding clouds. As Mr. Lincoln, with his tall, gaunt form, stepped out, he lifted his hand to silence the cheering throng. For a moment he waited, as though memories were stirring his emotions, and then in a firm, clear voice, somewhat shrill and yet with an inexpressible pathos in it, he began his address. Just as he did so, through a rift in the clouds the sun shone full upon him. The clouds parted further, until the whole of the sky above was clear. To the crowd it was an omen, and Lincoln said later that he sensed it, too.

As his Address ended there was a moment of utter silence, and then applause; and the reception accorded him as he concluded was marked as much by tears as it was by cheers, for according to the reports of those present even the applause had in it a note of solemnity.

The Address, when published, was variously received. However, no appraisal of it can be quite as informative to us as the one which Lincoln himself made. Some ten days after his inauguration the President wrote a letter to a friend, the journalist Thurlow Weed, of New York. He said:

> Dear Mr. Weed:
>
> Every one likes a compliment. Thank you for yours on my little notification speech and on the recent inaugural address. I expect the latter to wear as well as, perhaps better than, anything I have produced; but I believe it is not immediately popular. Men are not flattered by being shown that there has been a difference of purpose between the

> Almighty and them. To deny it, however, in this case, is to deny that there is a God governing the world. It is a truth I thought needed to be told, and, as whatever of humiliation there is in it falls most directly on myself, I thought others might afford for me to tell it.

Gladstone declared that he had been "taken captive" by the President's composition. "I see in it", he said, "the effect of sharp trial, when rightly borne, to raise men to higher level of thought and action. . . . Lincoln's words show that upon him anxiety have wrought their true effect."

The Second Inaugural contains the words of a man whose heart was deeply stirred, of a man who, without conscious thought of art or artifice, rose to heights of artless art. In his phrases there is something of the wild, capricious poetry of human life. His words are unsurpassed for simple beauty, dignity and grandeur. They are lofty, manly, and Christian in their sentiment. Lincoln always was powerful when he felt that he was right. His whole nature responded to the appeal of Justice. In this instance he was so well convinced that he was battling for truth and right that he was irresistible. It was the great heart of the wise and humble leader which gave us this gospel of concentrated truth, and with a crystal clarity and a rhythm of emotion that makes it well-nigh blank verse poetry. The scriptural cadences are freighted with a moral intensity.

It is easy enough to read this Address, and to approve it; but if you wish to wonder at it, think yourself back into 1865, when hate, and fear, and prejudice, and bigotry, and intolerance stalked the Land. In spite of such conditions, Lincoln kept his head. He never once appealed to prejudice or intolerance, or to unfairness of any kind. Ten years before, Lincoln had written to his friend Joshua F. Speed, concerning the Know-Nothing Party which was then campaigning up and down the countryside making its appeals to ignorance and to prejudice. Lincoln might have availed himself of their support, yet his whole attitude was expressed in this letter:

> How can anyone who abhors the oppression of negroes be in favor of degrading classes of white people? Our progress

in degeneracy appears to me to be pretty rapid. As a nation, we began by declaring that "all men are created equal except negroes." When the Know-Nothings get control, it will read, "all men are created equal except negroes and foreigners and Catholics." When it comes to this, I shall prefer emigrating to some country where they make no pretense of loving liberty—to Russia, for instance, where despotism can be taken pure, and without the base alloy of hypocrisy.

Again he had said, at the Republican Convention of 1856: "Let us appeal to the sense and patriotism of the people, not to their prejudices; let us spread the floods of enthusiasm here aroused all over these vast prairies so suggestive of freedom. There is both a power and a magic in popular opinion. To that let us now appeal."

In Cincinnati, and answering a question as to what he would do to those who opposed him if he were elected, he said: "We mean to remember that you are as good as we: that there is no difference between us other than the difference of circumstances. We mean to recognize and bear in mind always that you have as good hearts in your bosom as other people, or as we claim to have, and treat you accordingly."

On the night of his election for a second term, he responded to a crowd of serenaders: "If I know my heart, my gratitude is free from any taint of personal triumph. I do not impugn the motives of anyone opposed to me."

More books have been written about Lincoln than about anybody else who ever lived, excepting Jesus only. In many respects Lincoln bears a character-resemblance to our Saviour. Lincoln was an Overcomer all his life. He got the better of circumstances; he conquered difficulties and opposition; he won despite his handicaps, and he left an entire heritage for posterity. The elements of his bigness include his analytical mind, his strong intelligence, his ability to state a proposition with clarity and exactness; his faith in man and God; his never-failing sense of humor, his true sense of proportion, his powers of persuasion in public speaking;

his kindliness, patience, fairness, and his simplicity and sincerity. These were all so much a part of Lincoln that it seems inevitable that he should win his way from rail-splitter to flatboatman, to storekeeper, to postmaster, to county surveyor, to a captaincy in the Black Hawk War, to three terms in the legislature of Illinois, to a term in the Congress of the United States, to the position of accepted political leader, to a national reputation as a lawyer, to the Presidency of the United States.

Lincoln overcame calumny with kindness. Those who hated the things for which he stood, hated him and reviled him, and persecuted him and said all manner of evil things against him. They called him a "mulatto", a "buffoon", a "monster", an "idiot", a "traitor", an "agitator", a "radical", a "baboon". But Lincoln never allowed the thunder of calumny and scorn to sour the milk of human kindness within his nature. He mastered those who opposed him. He was patient with their impatience. He laughed at their hysteria. Calamity-howling he confronted with calmness, and pugnacious emotionalism with serenity; and perfidy with poise; and biting, critical opposition with magnanimity. When a visitor at the White House told Lincoln that Stanton, his Secretary of War, had called the President a "damned fool", Lincoln said: "Well, Stanton is generally right. I'll have to look into this." He so mastered the men who at first opposed him that, after four years of opportunity to measure him for size, Edwin McMasters Stanton, speaking for them all, said as he stood beside the dead President: "There lies the most perfect ruler of men the world has ever seen."

One source of Lincoln's power of overcoming, all through his life, was his faith in God. He was profoundly and sincerely a man of faith. It was this that enabled him to withstand the storms of ghastly cataclysm, and the political intrigues that beat upon him. It enabled him to see the long course of history to which his single life and this vast world belong. He felt himself to be in tune with the Almighty Who encompasses all centuries and all places in His infinite mind and purpose. It was this that enabled him to stand above all bigotry and intolerance, and to address himself, to all humanity, in words that are and always will remain sublime. The scriptural cadences of the Second Inaugural are freighted with moral purpose. And when he came to his concluding sentence he gave expression to a sentiment which should find lodgment in every leader's mind and heart today:

> With malice toward none, with charity for all, with firmness in the right as God gives us to see the right, let us strive on to finish the work we are in, to bind up the nation's wounds, to care for him who shall have borne the battle and for his widow and orphans, to do all which may achieve and cherish a just and a lasting peace among ourselves and with all nations.

The Road Away from Revolution

In these doubtful and anxious days, when all the world is at unrest and, look which way you will, the road ahead seems darkened by shadows which portend dangers of many kinds, it is only common prudence that we should look about us and attempt to assess the causes of distress and the most likely means of removing them. There must be some real ground for the universal unrest and perturbation. It is not to be found in superficial politics or in mere economic blunders.

But the mistakes which have been made need not be repeated, and we can move on towards right ends by right means, if only we think clearly and act unselfishly.

The sum of the whole mtter is, that our civilization cannot survive materially unless it be redeemed spiritually. It cn be saved only by becoming permeated with the spirit of Christ and being made free and happy by the practices which spring out of that spirit. Only thus can dislontent be driven out and all the shadows lifted from the road ahead.

Here is the final challenge to our churches, to our political organizations, and to our capitalists. Shall we not all earnestly cooperate to bring in the new day?

Finale 9

To the sentence "Here is the final challenge" &c. add, after the word capitalists, a comma and dash and the words — to everyone who fears God or loves his country.

W.W.

The road that leads away from revolution is clearly marked, for it is defined by the nature of men and of organized society.

Woodrow Wilson's "The Road Away from Revolution"

[7]

MANY ESSAYS, many epistles, have been written on Americanism, but one which I believe posterity a hundred and two hundred years hence will place along with the other writings included in this volume is the last article that Woodrow Wilson ever wrote.

With the exception of Abraham Lincoln, Woodrow Wilson had the keenest analytical mind that has ever occupied the White House. With the exception of George Washington and Abraham Lincoln, he stands without a peer as a patriot among our Presidents. Wilson was reviled and persecuted, vilified and lied about, but no more than were Washington and Lincoln in their days. For excellence of literary style, for incisiveness of thought and clarity of expression, he stands unsurpassed, except by Lincoln.

He was a child of the parsonage, and throughout his life the moral purposes and the Christian ideals of his Presbyterian preacher-father held sway over him. His preparation for world leadership in an hour of crisis was well-nigh perfect. Born in Virginia, brought up in the deeper South and educated in the North, he had a sympathetic understanding of our national history which, added to his keen powers of analysis, made him one of the most discriminating historians American scholarship has produced. As college professor, as university president, as governor of New Jersey, as President of the United States, he increased in mental stature and held fast to his ideals.

As President, he showed his strength of leadership in keeping America out of war as long as he did, and then when America finally was drawn in, his intellectual powers and spiritual insight served the whole world well; for it was Woodrow Wilson who, when the war had wallowed its bloody way across Europe for two full years, seized it and lifted the whole ugly business out of the sordid and the commercial and the revengeful and put it on the high plane of moral purpose, and articulated the ideals of the United States in entering it, and pursuing it to its end.

Although those ideals were lost in the long-continued and paralyzing discouragements and diplomatic defeats that followed, Wilson stood fast to the doctrines of peace and justice and the settlement of disputes by conference and understanding on the basis of international good will. He held fast to what he had voiced when the whole world was acclaiming him as its spokesman-leader.

Following his break in health and his retirement from the White House, Wilson was not able to carry on his more vigorous activities. Nevertheless, he kept mentally alert to what was happening. Mrs. Wilson tells us that in the spring of 1923 the former President began to display a sense of anxiety over the turn of affairs within the Nation. He seemed to have a premonition of the troubles that finally burst upon us in 1929 and would ultimately place in jeopardy the very fabric of the Republic. He expressed a wish to write an article, but he had only the use of his right hand. Moreover, a return of neuritis in that hand was making it all but impossible for him to hold a pen. He turned to his typewriter, but could pick out the letters only with the greatest difficulty. So he began to dictate to Mrs. Wilson what he wanted to say. Slowly, sometimes giving a single sentence in the middle of the night, sometimes in the midst of relaxation dictating another phrase, Wilson finally completed a short article that he called THE ROAD AWAY FROM REVOLUTION. He polished it again and again, smoothing its diction, sharpening its style, making certain that it said what he wanted it to say. He sent it to *The Atlantic Monthly,* and it was published.

The text is a warning against trends of selfishness and materialism in the Nation, even as were the Epistles of Paul against the evils that were manifesting themselves in the church at Corinth. He spoke of the universal unrest, and instead of denouncing everybody who talked about it he pleaded for a removal of its causes. These causes, as he considered them, lay deeper than "mere economic blunders" or "superficial politics". His text impeached the "whole social system". Have the men of business, he asked, "generally used their power for the benefit of the countries in which their capital is employed and for the benefit of their fellow men?" He re-evoked the gospel of service and unselfishness, and in a way that would prompt certain "red baiters" to dub as "communist" anyone who said the same things today. He faced the situation as he saw it, and presented his analysis for the consideration of those who might avoid its consequences.

Woodrow Wilson's patriotism and Americanism will stand the severest tests of time. He was an American of the Americans. He was a patriot whose patriotism during his own lifetime was tested as by fire. It would be well were we to listen to the plea he made, to his call for "a Christian conception of justice", and to not pass lightly over his reference to "the too great selfishness of the capitalistic system." Here are the memorable words of his conclusion:

> The sum of the whole matter is this, that our civilization cannot survive materially unless it be redeemed spiritually. It can be saved only by becoming permeated with the spirit of Christ and being made free and happy by the practices which spring out of that spirit. Only thus can discontent be driven out and all the shadows lifted from the road ahead.
>
> Here is the final challenge to our churches, to our political organizations, and to our capitalists—to everyone who fears God or loves his country. Shall we not all earnestly co-operate to bring in the new day?

Wilson issued his challenge to our churches, to our political organizations, and to our men of business, industry and finance, summoning them to intelligently cooperate in ushering in that new day. May it not be that the stress and strain of the bewildering world conditions which are confronting us are but the birth throes of a new era, struggling for definition? Whether this new era is a potency for good or evil depends upon whether it is to be created selfishly or unselfishly; that is to say, whether it is to be Christian or, in the terms of Marx, materialistic. The spiritual concept of all human life is the only thing that can save humanity and its society from a recrudescence of the jungle. Belief is important. A wrong head invariably eventuates from a wrong heart. A materialistic concept of life breeds low aims, selfishness, revenge. It is the essence of the "class-struggle".

President Wilson accepted the capitalist system as a logical one. And he would have this system continue, and perpetuate itself with honor and responsibility, in the coming day. But he would caution us that the old motivation of greed and revenge and selfishness and overreaching is doomed, as surely as there is a God.

What was Wilson's alternative? Discontent, he wrote, can be driven out, and shadows lifted from the road ahead, by permeating civilization with the "spirit of Christ", and "by the practices which spring out of that spirit." Christ's standard of greatness was "whosoever would be chief among you, let him be your servant." To compete for first place after the manner of Jesus is to serve, for the only true greatness is in service. When this rule obtains, men will point with pride to their industries and their business enterprises, not because they pay so much in annual dividends but because they consciously participate in the artistry of human welfare.

Woodrow Wilson's bequest is of the "spirit of Christ". THE ROAD AWAY FROM REVOLUTION is for men to strive, early and late, that they may gain for themselves while consciously they help others to find a richer, fuller life.

My fellow Countrymen:

Today the guns are silent. A great tragedy has ended. A great victory has been won. An entire world lies quietly at peace. The skies no longer rain death, the seas bear only commerce; men everywhere walk upright in the sunlight. The holy mission entrusted to us has been completed. And in reporting this to you, the people, I speak for the thousands of silent lips forever stilled among the jungles and the beaches which marked the way; ~~[illegible]~~ I speak for the unnamed brave millions homeward bound to take up the challenge of that future which they did so much to salvage from the brink of disaster.

As I look back on that long, tortuous trail from those grim days of Bataan and Corregidor, when an entire world lived in fear; when democracy was on the defensive everywhere, when modern civilization trembled in the balance, I thank a merciful God that he has given us the faith, the courage and the power from which to mould victory. We have known the bitterness of defeat and the exultation of triumph and from both we have learned there can be no turning back; we must go forward to preserve in peace what we have won in war.

A new era is upon us. The lesson of victory itself brings with it profound concern. ~~for the future survival of civilization itself.~~ The destructiveness of the war potential has reached a point which involves the future survival of civilization itself

A new Era is upon us.

Douglas MacArthur's Address on the Occasion of the Surrender of Japan

[8]

IN OUR SEARCH for the roots of true Americanism we have found eight documents, their authors individually and collectively, and the aggregate of the external conditions and influences affecting the creation of the documents chosen. The eighth—and last—of these documents is the address which General Douglas MacArthur directed to his fellow countrymen at the formal surrender of Japan on board the United States battleship *Missouri,* on Sunday, September 2nd, 1945.

The man who had been appointed by the President of the United States to receive the surrender, and who had been approved by all the Allied Governments, was General Douglas MacArthur. With the exception of George Washington, MacArthur was undoubtedly the greatest and most distinguished military man the United States has ever produced. He was a professional career soldier, yet in character and mentality he was even more: he was a truly great man.

Douglas MacArthur has the distinction of having been graduated from the Military Academy at West Point with the highest academic grades ever achieved by any student in the one hundred and sixty-five years' history of that famous school. He was graduated on June 11, 1903, with highest honors, and immediately entered into the service of his Country.

When the United States was forced into World War I MacArthur was one of the first Army officers to achieve distinction. He helped to form the Forty-Second "Rainbow" Division, and gave it its name, from the fact that its men came from every section of the Nation, North, East, South and West. In a short time he became the great commander of that renowned Division.

Later he was sent to the Philippine Islands, where he was to win immortal fame. Here, after the United States' entry into the second world war, he became America's supreme representative in the vast operations in the Pacific and the Far East. It is a thrilling story, and the campaigns which took place under his command will be studied for generations to come.

The defeat of Japan was absolute and complete, and Douglas MacArthur became not only the United States appointee to receive the formal surrender; he at the same time was made Supreme Commander in charge of the restoration of Japan to the work and tasks of peace. His powers were practically dictatorial, yet he worked smoothly, diplomatically and successfully with and through the Emperor and the officers and officials of Japan. He helped the people and nation on their way to a firm and healthy *renaissance.*

MacArthur knew full well that the Emperor was the spiritual as well as the temporal ruler of Japan, and he worked with and through him, leaving his royal person untouched. He invited Hirohito to the American Embassy for a talk, and when the Emperor took himself to MacArthur's office the people of Japan saw that he, too, was subject to the Supreme Commander just as was the most humble gatherer of their rice. Then, two months after he had taken charge, MacArthur abolished the state religion, Shintoism, and thus at one move both lessened the time-honored authority of the Emperor and brought the people one step closer to the theory of the separation of church and state. In this step, too, he began a removal of the mythology, the legends, and the paganism which for generations had been teaching that the Emperor was the Son of Heaven, and divine, that his predecessors all were gods, and that the origin of the empire itself was divine. Shinto, MacArthur knew, was largely responsible for the zeal with which Japan was seeking to rule all Asia; it taught that one day Japan would succeed, and so instilled in the empire's subjects the belief that the highest service they could render was to die in the cause of the empire's destiny.

A fatal blow to this exalted concept was dealt on New Year's Day of 1946 when Emperor Hirohito spoke over the radio to the people of Japan and told them that their Emperor was not divine; that the ties which had bound the royal succession and his subjects were based on ancient legends; and that these myths were predicated upon the false conception that an emperor was divine, and upon an equally false doctrine that the Japanese were superior to other races and were destined to rule the world. Here was an example of sheer courage, to thus address an entire people and to shatter what for generations they had been taught was sacred. It was a gesture of magnificence, urged upon the Emperor by MacArthur, and in performing it Emperor Hirohito surely matched MacArthur's greatness. He had removed the props of militarism in his nation, and had shown the way to national peace and dignity.

The Supreme Commander went on with his quiet reformation, even ruling out what the Japanese called *Kempei-Tai,* the secret police which for centuries had pried into the people's most private thoughts and actions.

For over five years MacArthur dominated the Japanese scene. He destroyed Japan's military power; introduced representative democracy into the government; liberated the farmers, the tillers of the paddies and the soil; encouraged a free economy and a free labor movement; liberalized education; enfranchised the women of Japan; abolished police oppression, and brought about a division and distribution of the political powers of the state.

When to his service to Japan is added the amazing and unforgettable service he rendered to the people of the Philippine Islands, and the quietude he was bringing so successfully to the Far East when his noble career was ended, MacArthur emerges as the only professional soldier whose character, achievements and faith, whose doctrines and undiluted Americanism, and whose unfeigned patriotism and love of Country justify unreservedly the inclusion of the immortal address to his fellow countrymen from the battleship *Missouri,* in distant Tokyo Bay.

In remolding Japan from an absolute monarchy to a representative form of government; from a ruthless, war-mongering oligarchy into a peace-striving people and nation, he won the undying admiration and affection of the people of Japan. Seldom, if ever in history, has a conquered nation so mourned the peaceful departure of its conqueror as did the millions of Cipangu when MacArthur was called home.

The General was a stern and strict disciplinarian, yet at the same time he was a man of honesty and of fairness, of mercy and of compassion. A close student of his life would be fully justified in concluding that MacArthur experienced self-realization morally in terms of both the science and the practice of right conduct, and religiously in terms of fellowship with God.

One of his biographers has recounted this anecdote of him: "An old colonel who served several years under MacArthur summed up the staff opinion of the man thus: 'Douglas MacArthur is a hard-boiled old softie.' "

From the group of vessels assembled in the waters of Tokyo Bay on that September morning of surrender, all thoughts and eyes were on the battleship *Missouri.* It was MacArthur's day! His personality dominated every moment and every movement.

He was a handsome man, five feet ten inches tall, and always meticulously dressed. His speaking voice was clear and impressive, and he had a literary style that could have been envied by almost any public figure in the world. When the hour of ceremony struck, MacArthur came out on deck and stepped up to the microphone. He ordered the unfurling of the Flag, and then, the salute rendered, he began to speak. He spoke impressively, describing firmly the purpose for which they were assembled, namely, "to conclude a solemn agreement whereby Peace may be restored."

He went on, to express his own, and personal, aspirations: "It is my earnest hope," he said, "and indeed the hope of all mankind that from this solemn occasion a better world shall emerge out of the blood and carnage of the past—a world founded upon faith and understanding—a world dedicated to the dignity of man and the fulfillment of his most cherished wish—for freedom, tolerance and justice."

On board the ships of war was utter silence, even as silence reigned among the countless millions to whom the words were coming over the ether waves:

"As Supreme Commander for the Allied Powers I announce it my firm purpose, in the tradition of the countries I represent, to proceed in the discharge of my responsibilities with justice and tolerance, while taking all necessary dispositions to insure that the terms of surrender are fully, promptly and faithfully complied with."

Upon a signal from MacArthur, the Japanese delegates signed the terms of surrender, and then General MacArthur signed the document and then the representatives of the Allied Powers. The epochal document was complete.

When the ceremony of surrender ended General MacArthur broadcast to the American people the words which are now placed alongside Washington's Farewell Address, Lincoln's Second Inaugural, and the Compact that had been signed on board another ship, the tiny *Mayflower*, three hundred and twenty-five years before. The Supreme Commander began with these six short sentences:

> Today the guns are silent. A great tragedy has ended. A great victory has been won. The skies no longer rain death—the seas bear only commerce—men everywhere walk upright in the sunlight. The entire world lies quietly at Peace. The Holy Mission has been completed.

And now he was speaking directly to his fellow citizens, and asking them to look back, for a moment, to the time "when an entire world lived in fear; when Democracy was on the defensive everywhere, when modern civilization trembled in the balance . . ."

And then he paused an instant, and said: "I thank a merciful God that He has given us the faith, the courage and the power from which to mould victory."

He drew the world's attention to the destructiveness of war's new potential, alluding to the awesome achievements of science and doubtless—though he did not mention it—to the atomic bomb that had been dropped on Hiroshima. He spoke of the universal hunger for peace. He observed that military alliances, balances of power, and even the League of Nations, had failed, all of them. He lamented the fact that these failures had seemed to leave to the nations only "the crucible of war" as the ultimate recourse in the settlement of their differences. Then he posed directly today's great human challenge: "The utter destructiveness of war," he said, "now blots out this alternative." Humanity itself faced the ultimate in horror; and MacArthur, even as scores of distinguished military men had done before him, pleaded for an end to the futility, and the destructiveness, of armed conflict.

William Tecumseh Sherman, one of the greatest generals of the Civil War and the man whose march through Georgia had left behind it a wake of desolation, was one of those who pleaded similarly. Fourteen years after that war was ended Sherman was making an address to the graduating class of the Michigan Military Academy, and he said: "I am tired and sick of war. Its glory is all moonshine. It is only those who have neither fired a shot nor heard the shrieks and groans of the wounded, who cry aloud for blood, more vengeance, more desolation. War is hell."

Now came the section in MacArthur's address which reveals the deep intensity of his religious faith, and his utter conviction of war's ultimate futility. Possibly because Mrs. MacArthur was Episcopalian the General had joined the Episcopal Church, but his ancestry was out of Scotland and his forebears of the famous old Scotch Presbyterian faith. The word "covenant" was big with historical meaning to them, for they and their kind had covenanted to defend the Creed. To those of the beliefs of John Calvin there is awesome meaning in the book of REVELATION (16:14–16), when "the spirits of devils . . . go forth unto the kings of the earth and of the whole world, to gather them to the battle of that great day of God Almighty." Here there would be a pouring out of howls of wrath, and there would be a great slaughter, a ruinous misadventure and disastrous finality. All this would come to be in "a place called in the Hebrew tongue Armageddon."

Untold millions were listening, at their radios, as MacArthur's words came to them from the deck of the *Missouri*: "We have had our last chance. If we do not devise some greater and more equitable system Armageddon will be at our door."

"The problem basically is theological," he continued, "and involves a spiritual recrudescence and improvement of human character that will synchronize with our almost matchless advance in science, art, literature and all material and cultural developments of the past two thousand years. It must be of the spirit if we are to save the flesh."

MacArthur, too, was speaking unto the generations.

In Conclusion

[9]

THE THOUGHTS, the ideas, and the aspirations that are set forth in these eight writings differ as much from one another in their expression as do the books of the Bible. Those which finally were included in the Sacred Volume were put there because they measured up to certain standards; and because they were repositories of religious truth. They revealed God to man, and man's dependence upon God, and the working out of God's divine will among all the children of men. So, too, in the present volume, one hears a theme which binds these writings as by a golden thread, America's spirit, the genius of America itself.

A divine drive of purposive idealism breathes through all of them. From their entirety is to be discovered what America is, for all of them, and each one separately, have sprung from the deepest roots of our true heritage and mission. And the American Republic, as James Russell Lowell so sapiently said in reply to the French historian Guizot, will endure "as long as the ideas of the men who founded it continue dominant."

It is important that the ideas and the ideals of the founding fathers of our Nation be rehearsed to each new generation, and especially to the present younger generation for that generation is confronted with a challenge that one may term magnificent. *They* have not made that challenge, yet it faces them; and they must choose between its alternatives—two irreconcilably divergent theories of society and government.

On the one hand is the old, totalitarian state, in all its modern dress. In it the powers and responsibilities of government are precisely focused in one person or entity. The dictator may have waded to his seat of power through crimson seas of carnage; and he may have achieved his power by the vote and acquiescence of his people. He holds his power, nonetheless, by physical force and violence, even though these may be cloaked in legal raiment. Liberty of opinion does not exist. The firing squad and the concentration camp put the quietus upon freedom of speech and of the press. The pulpit is subservient to the whim of the state, and is required to render unto Caesar the things that are rightfully God's. Education is trammeled to serve the ends of an ideological authority, fawning before the flattery of its adherents and cringing before their denunciation. Bigotry and intolerance, proscription and persecution, all are invoked in the name of the people's welfare, and are accepted under its illusion, and chained to its efficiency.

On the other hand is a new and youthful theory, the representative republic. It may not be as efficient at a given moment as are the older forms, yet the only way for a people to develop, and to progress individually and as a society, is for them to shoulder the responsibilities of directing their own affairs, of shaping their own objectives, and of determining their own progress within the society which they themselves have formed. The claimed efficiency of the totalitarian state can be purchased, yes; but it is purchased at a price which no sane people ever voluntarily pay.

Our Republic rests upon a theory which is revolutionary in all of history. That theory had been voiced by wise men and philosophers throughout the ages, yet it remained for the men of the Constitutional Convention to honorably put it into practice, and to give it viability in its form. The theory states that governments derive their just powers only from the consent of the governed. It holds that government is made for man, not man to serve the government. It assumes that people need institutions, and that in time of institutional crisis the people themselves will save, or modify, or remake their institutions of their own free will. It is a theory that protects the liberty of one's opinion, the freedom of speech of the individual and of the press, for these are its very breath and life. It guarantees the free, untrammeled exercise of religious faith, for religion inheres in the most intimate nature of man and is vital and intelligent only when it is called forth by the experiences of daily life. This theory, *per se,* safeguards the freedom of the pulpit, learning therefrom its moral sense of direction. It defends the academic freedom of the schools, recognizing that our Republic's continuing and fundamental challenge is to develop an intelligence equal to the social responsibility of its citizenry, for history tells us that in the course of time men are likely to regard the democratic institutions of their communities as ends in themselves, keeping them static instead of dynamic, and coming to hold the recorded parchments of their history as more valid than are the principles which gave them being.

Through the roots of true Americanism there flows the spirit of tolerance, and in them no place is accorded prejudice, whether it be racial, religious, social or otherwise. Democracy in America is an attitude of mind, a condition of man's soul.

This was the democracy that was paramount in the minds of the men who founded the Republic, and one of the greatest of our present difficulties stems from the fact that many of us have come to think of democracy as a *mechanism* of government. Representative democracy, however, is a spirit that finds its sanction in man's inalienable nature. Man was *meant* to be free. True Americanism is operable only in a state of society in which government is dedicated to the service of human freedom and has for its supreme aim the furtherance of human progress. In our American system, government has been conceived as the servant of the people, subject always to the people's enlightened will. With us, power is responsibility, and that responsibility, for as long as the Republic shall endure, devolves upon *us,* each one.

Equality of opportunity and equality before the law are essential to our concept of nationhood. Carved in the marble over the entrance to the magnificent home of the Supreme Court of the United States are these four words: EQUAL JUSTICE UNDER LAW. This is the hope and prayer of every true American.

Education is another need that is made apparent by a study of the foundations of the American Republic. And let me stress that I am using the word "education" in its broadest, most comprehensive sense, for *unregimented education* is the one thing that the fascist, the communist, or the subversive intellectual most fears. The ideas which they represent are anathema to the overwhelming majority of our people, yet if we become too preoccupied with their damnation we are flouting every lesson of ideological history. You cannot kill an idea by damning, imprisoning, making martyrs of or shooting those who hold it. The way to get rid of an idea is to offer a better one, and the one sure way to disseminate right ideas is to inculcate them through education.

Such ideas are reflected in these great documents. In them lies one of the greatest contributions to human progress ever made, a magnificent, historic step toward realization of the age-long dream of all mankind, the dream that man may come to live a life of dignity and freedom, and to participate equally with his fellows in the supreme art of his own self-government. We, of all peoples, must cherish them, honor their rightful place in the world's great treasury of the humanities, and put them in the forefront of all our schools' curricula. As President Howard has remarked in his cogent FOREWORD: "No citizen who loves freedom is truly literate while unfamiliar with these writings." And, while filling the mind with the doctrine of true Americanism, the intelligent patriot will try earnestly to remove the causes of social discontent.

No people's rule over itself is safe unless there is intelligence, morality, character, and a deep, abiding faith in God. When a people undertake to do their own self-governing they assume the responsibilities as well as the privileges of what they have undertaken. Therefore education must be as widely diffused as is the right of suffrage, for only an intelligent people is fit to govern itself. Education must inculcate a sense of values, for when a people has a sense of moral direction it is equipped to take into its own hands the helm of its Ship of State, and then to keep her straight and steady upon her course.

The authors of the Mayflower Compact declared that they would enact just and equal laws, and solemnly pledged themselves to give due and reverent obedience to those laws. Reverence for law stands out from every fibre that has been woven into the fabric of true Americanism. Abraham Lincoln has described it:

> Let every American, every lover of liberty, every well-wisher of his posterity, swear by the blood of the Revolution never to violate in the least particular the laws of the country, and never to tolerate their violation by others. As the patriots of Seventy-Six did to the support of the Declaration of Independence, so to the support of the Constitution and the laws let every American pledge his life, his property, and his sacred honor. Let every man remember that to violate the law is to trample on the blood of his fathers and to tear the charter of his own and his children's liberty. Let reverence for the laws be breathed by every American mother to the lisping babe that prattles on her lap; let it be taught in schools, in seminaries, and in colleges; let it be written in primers, spelling books and almanacs; let it be preached from the pulpits, proclaimed in the legislative halls, and enforced in courts of justice. In short, let it become the political religion of the nation.

There can be no true liberty without limitations, no true freedom without a recognition of restricting responsibilities, no true Americanism without personal self-control. Socrates called morality the art of self-possession and self-government. The one fundamental virtue, he taught, was "rule over oneself." And obedience is by no means synonymous with subservience or subordination.

One has seen, again and again, throughout the writings in this book, that a regnant idea of the men who fashioned the Republic was freedom to worship God. The reverse side of this was their own personal faith in God. They worshiped God, they wanted others to enjoy untrammeled the right to worship Him. And any right, if it is to be sustained, must be exercised. Our fathers worshiped

God because they believed in Him. Their lives were God-centered. Their faith lent to all their work an unspeakable solemnity and a moral significance.

They believed in prayer, and expressed their belief not only in their words but by praying daily and devoutly to the Almighty.

They believed in the Holy Bible. Our great American leaders, from the beginning to the present, almost without exception, have been faithful to its precepts. What George Washington said would have been approved by almost every one of his compatriots: "Above all, the pure and benign light of Revelation has had a meliorating influence on mankind, and increased the blessings of society."

Nearly all of those who have shaped the American spirit would say, with Ulysses Simpson Grant:

> Hold fast to the Bible as the sheet anchor of your liberties; write its precepts on your hearts and practice them in your lives. To the influence of this Book we are indebted for the progress made in civilization, and to this we must look as our guide in the future.

These expressions are not exceptional; they are typical of the belief of the greatest of our Americans.

They voice the thoughts, the ideals and the aspirations of a people.

They are the gossamer thread of America's spirit, the genius of America itself.

Epilogue

[10]

"GREAT MEN hallow a whole people, and lift up all that live in their time." So declared Sydney Smith, a famous English preacher, author and wit of a century and a half ago. The word he employed was a strong one, for *hallow* is far more profoundly meaningful than any of its synonyms.

The men who have been chosen, in questing for the roots of true Americanism, were, all of them, great men. Each one contributed a document without which this symposium of Americanism would be a great deal less meaningful than it is. These documents endure, and dare, and hallow the whole of our people and Nation.

The first three were the products of groups of such men, groups whose members were bound together by the most lofty of purposes and ideals. I like to think, figuratively, of their achievements, as the building, and furnishing, and safe-guarding of our Temple of Liberty and Self-Government.

Thus, the men who wrote the Mayflower Compact, and who guided their own lives by it, laid the corner-stone of the Temple of Liberty which is our Republic.

The men who adopted and then victoriously honored the Declaration of Independence constructed the adamantine framework of the Temple.

The men who devised, created and then adopted the Constitution of these United States erected the stately Temple of our puissant Nation.

Among the thousands whose words and deeds reflect the stateliness of that Temple there are five, it seems to me, who have made such vital, intelligent and dynamic contributions to the understanding of its significance, that each must have his special niche in the eternal Shrine of our Americanism.

The first of these is George Washington. To him was entrusted the first chief custodianship of our Nation's Temple of Liberty and Self-Government, and in the discharge of that trust he gave a total and sacrificial devotion, an utter dedication; and in the discharge of his responsibilities there was not a single instance of equivocation. And then, toward the end of his magnificent life, the Congress of the United States, on the 19th of December, 1799, confirmed by Resolution his place in all our heritage: "First in war, first in peace, and first in the hearts of his countrymen. . . ."

Within the Temple was its liturgy, and Francis Scott Key enriched and then exalted it by giving to it a song that set the bells ringing, and the drums beating, and the bugles blowing, and the people singing—

'Tis the Star-spangled banner! O long may it wave
O'er the land of the free and the home of the brave!

Abraham Lincoln, by refusing to call wrong right, saved the Temple from destruction; and when he led the majority of the people to its salvation he assured the lesser numbers that they—and *all* Americans—would be secure in their Temple of Liberty and Self-Government, "With malice toward none, with charity for all . . ."

The next is Woodrow Wilson, whose knowledge and whose philosophy of history make him the most authentic prophet of our time. Our civilization, he warned, "cannot survive materially unless it is redeemed spiritually"; "Only thus can discontent be driven out" of the Temple, and "all the shadows lifted" from the roads that lead to it, and the skies themselves become translucent above the Shrine of Liberty and Self-Government.

Now comes the climactic finishing of the Temple, and above it reach its tower and its spire. The Temple, itself a symbol, is formed of all the loyal citizenry of the Nation, rich and poor alike. Its tower reflects the vital, intelligent patriotism of the finest of our people, for patriotism is one of the most noble impulses of good men.

In these hours of stress, of threat, of challenge, may each citizen of America gaze at the structure which his forebears have bequeathed, and of which he himself is now a part. And as he hearkens back to the words of Washington and the others, and as he reads verbatim the documents to which allusion has been made, may he be inspired by the life of our great contemporary, General of the Army Douglas MacArthur, who could have said, with Sir Cecil Spring-Rice:

> I vow to thee, my country—all earthly things above—
> Entire and whole and perfect, the service of my love . . .

Sturdy and strong, the Temple, and above its altarpiece are writ the words which were spoken to its congregation at a moment of history, from Tokyo Bay:

> It must be of the spirit if we are to save the flesh.

Heavenward, from the sturdy tower, a slender spire arises; an index finger pointing upward, unto God, and unto the generations.

THE APPENDIX

THE MAYFLOWER COMPACT

In y^e name of God, Amen. We whose names are underwriten, the loyall subjects of our dread soveraigne Lord, King James, by y^e grace of God, of Great Britaine, Franc, & Ireland king, defender of ye faith, &c., haveing undertaken, for ye glorie of God, and advancemente of ye Christian faith, and honour of our king & countrie, a voyage to plant ye first colonie in ye Northerne parts of Virginia, doe by these presents solemnly & mutualy in ye presence of God, and one of another, covenant & combine our selves togeather into a civill body politick, for our better ordering & preservation & furtherance of ye ends aforesaid; and by vertue hearof to enacte, constitute, and frame such just & equall lawes, ordinances, acts, constitutions, & offices, from time to time, as shall be thought most meete & convenient for ye generall good of ye Colonie, unto which we promise all due submission and obedience. In witnes wherof we have hereunder subscribed our names at Cap-Codd y^e 11. of November, in y^e year of y^e raigne of our soveraigne lord, King James, of England, France, & Ireland y^e eighteenth, and of Scotland y^e fiftie fourth. An^o: Dom. 1620.

In CONGRESS, July 4, 1776.

The unanimous Declaration of the thirteen united States of America,

WHEN in the Course of human events, it becomes necessary for one people to dissolve the political bands which have connected them with another, and to assume among the powers of the earth, the separate and equal station to which the Laws of Nature and of Nature's God entitle them, a decent respect to the opinions of mankind requires that they should declare the causes which impel them to the separation. ——— We hold these truths to be self-evident, that all men are created equal, that they are endowed by their Creator with certain unalienable Rights, that among these are Life, Liberty and the pursuit of Happiness. — That to secure these rights, Governments are instituted among Men, deriving their just powers from the consent of the governed, — That whenever any Form of Government becomes destructive of these ends, it is the Right of the People to alter or to abolish it, and to institute new Government, laying its foundation on such principles and organizing its powers in such form, as to them shall seem most likely to effect their Safety and Happiness. Prudence, indeed, will dictate that Governments long established should not be changed for light and transient causes; and accordingly all experience hath shewn, that mankind are more disposed to suffer, while evils are sufferable, than to right themselves by abolishing the forms to which they are accustomed. But when a long train of abuses and usurpations, pursuing invariably the same Object evinces a design to reduce them under absolute Despotism, it is their right, it is their duty, to throw off such Government, and to provide new Guards for their future security. — Such has been the patient sufferance of these Colonies; and such is now the necessity which constrains them to alter their former Systems of Government. The history of the present King of Great Britain is a history of repeated injuries and usurpations, all having in direct object the establishment of an absolute Tyranny over these States. To prove this, let Facts be submitted to a candid world. ———
He has refused his Assent to Laws, the most wholesome and necessary for the public good. —— He has forbidden his Governors to pass Laws of immediate and pressing importance, unless suspended in their operation till his Assent should be obtained; and when so suspended, he has utterly neglected to attend to them. —— He has refused to pass

other Laws for the accommodation of large districts of people, unless those people would relinquish the right of Representation in the Legislature, a right inestimable to them and formidable to tyrants only. —— He has called together legislative bodies at places unusual, uncomfortable, and distant from the depository of their public Records, for the sole purpose of fatiguing them into compliance with his measures. —— He has dissolved Representative Houses repeatedly, for opposing with manly firmness his invasions on the rights of the people. —— He has refused for a long time, after such dissolutions, to cause others to be elected; whereby the Legislative powers, incapable of Annihilation, have returned to the People at large for their exercise; the State remaining in the mean time exposed to all the dangers of invasion from without, and convulsions within. —— He has endeavoured to prevent the population of these States; for that purpose obstructing the Laws of Naturalization of Foreigners; refusing to pass others to encourage their migrations hither, and raising the conditions of new Appropriations of Lands. —— He has obstructed the Administration of Justice, by refusing his Assent to Laws for establishing Judiciary powers. —— He has made Judges dependent on his Will alone, for the tenure of their offices, and the amount and payment of their salaries. —— He has erected a multitude of New Offices, and sent hither swarms of Officers to harrass our people, and eat out their substance. —— He has kept among us, in times of peace, Standing Armies without the Consent of our legislatures. —— He has affected to render the Military independent of and superior to the Civil power. —— He has combined with others to subject us to a jurisdiction foreign to our constitution, and unacknowledged by our laws; giving his Assent to their Acts of pretended Legislation: — For quartering large bodies of armed troops among us: — For protecting them, by a mock Trial, from punishment for any Murders which they should commit on the Inhabitants of these States: — For cutting off our Trade with all parts of the world: — For imposing Taxes on us without our Consent: — For depriving us in many cases, of the benefits of Trial by Jury: — For transporting us beyond Seas to be tried for pretended offences: — For abolishing the free System of English Laws in a neighbouring Province, establishing therein an Arbitrary government, and enlarging its Boundaries so as to render it at once an example and fit instrument for introducing the same absolute rule into these Colonies: — For taking away our Charters, abolishing our most valuable Laws, and altering fundamentally the Forms of our Governments: — For suspending our own Legislatures, and declaring themselves invested with power to legislate for us in all cases whatsoever. —— He has abdicated Government here, by declaring us out of his Protection and waging War against us. —— He has plundered our seas, ravaged our Coasts, burnt our towns, and destroyed the lives of our people. —— He is at this time transporting large Armies of foreign Mercenaries to compleat the works of death, desolation and tyranny, already begun with circumstances of Cruelty & perfidy scarcely paralleled in the most barbarous ages, and totally unworthy the Head of a civilized nation. —— He has constrained our fellow Citizens taken Captive on the high Seas to bear Arms against their Country, to become the executioners of their friends and Brethren, or to fall themselves by their Hands. —— He has excited domestic insurrections amongst us, and has endeavoured to bring on the inhabitants of our frontiers, the merciless Indian Savages, whose known rule of warfare, is an undistinguished destruction of all ages, sexes and conditions. In every stage of these Oppressions We have Petitioned for Redress in the most humble terms: Our repeated Petitions have been answered only by repeated injury. A Prince, whose character is thus marked by every act which may define a Tyrant, is unfit to be the ruler of a free people. Nor have We been wanting in attentions to our Brittish brethren. We have warned them from time to time of attempts by their legislature to extend an unwarrantable jurisdiction over us. We have reminded them of the circumstances of our emigration and settlement here. We have appealed to their native justice and magnanimity, and we have conjured them by the ties of our common kindred to disavow these usurpations, which, would inevitably interrupt our connections and correspondence. They too have been deaf to the voice of justice and of consanguinity. We must, therefore, acquiesce in the necessity, which denounces our Separation, and hold them, as we hold the rest of mankind, Enemies in War, in Peace Friends. ——

We, therefore, the Representatives of the united States of America, in General Congress, Assembled, appealing to the Supreme Judge of the world for the rectitude of our intentions, do, in the Name, and by Authority of the good People of these Colonies, solemnly publish and declare, That these United Colonies are, and of Right ought to be Free and Independent States; that they are Absolved from all Allegiance to the British Crown, and that all political connection between them and the State of Great Britain, is and ought to be totally dissolved; and that as Free and Independent States, they have full Power to levy War, conclude Peace, contract Alliances, establish Commerce, and to do all other Acts and Things which Independent States may of right do. —— And for the support of this Declaration, with a firm reliance on the protection of divine Providence, we mutually pledge to each other our Lives, our Fortunes and our sacred Honor.

John Hancock

Button Gwinnett
Lyman Hall
Geo Walton.

Wm Hooper
Joseph Hewes,
John Penn

Edward Rutledge.
Thos Heyward Junr
Thomas Lynch Junr
Arthur Middleton

Samuel Chase
Wm Paca
Thos Stone
Charles Carroll
of Carrollton

George Wythe
Richard Henry Lee.
Th Jefferson

Benj^{a} Harrison
Thos Nelson jr.
Francis Lightfoot Lee
Carter Braxton

Robt Morris
Benjamin Rush
Benj^{a} Franklin
John Morton
Geo Clymer
Ja^{s} Smith.
Geo. Taylor
James Wilson
Geo. Ross

Caesar Rodney
Geo Read
Tho M: Kean

Wm Floyd
Phil. Livingston
Fran^{s} Lewis
Lewis Morris

Richd Stockton
Jno Witherspoon
Fra^{s} Hopkinson
John Hart
Abra Clark

Josiah Bartlett
Wm Whipple

Saml Adams
John Adams
Robt Treat Paine
Elbridge Gerry

Step. Hopkins
William Ellery

Roger Sherman
Saml Huntington
Wm Williams
Oliver Wolcott
Matthew Thornton

THE CONSTITUTION OF THE UNITED STATES

We the People of the United States, in Order to form a more perfect Union, establish Justice, insure domestic Tranquility, provide for the common defence, promote the general Welfare, and secure the Blessings of Liberty to ourselves and our Posterity, do ordain and establish this Constitution for the United States of America.

ARTICLE I

SECTION 1

All legislative Powers herein granted shall be vested in a Congress of the United States, which shall consist of a Senate and House of Representatives.

SECTION 2

The House of Representatives shall be composed of Members chosen every second Year by the People of the several States, and the Electors in each State shall have [the]* Qualifications requisite for Electors of the most numerous Branch of the State Legislature.

No Person shall be a Representative who shall not have attained to the Age of twenty five Years, and been seven Years a Citizen of the United States, and who shall not, when elected, be an Inhabitant of that State in which he shall be chosen.

Representatives and direct Taxes shall be apportioned among the several States which may be included within this Union, according to their respective Numbers, which shall be determined by adding to the whole Number of free Persons, including those bound to Service for a Term of Years, and excluding Indians not taxed, three fifths of all other Persons. The actual Enumeration shall be made within three Years after the first Meeting of the Congress of the United States, and within every subsequent Term of ten Years, in such Manner as they shall by Law direct. The Number of Representatives shall not exceed one for every thirty Thousand, but each State shall have at Least one Representative; and until such enumeration shall be made, the State

* The Word, "the," being interlined between the seventh and eighth Lines of the first Page, The word "Thirty" being partly written on an Erazure in the fifteenth Line of the first Page, The Words "is tried" being interlined between the thirty second and thirty third Lines of the first Page and the Word "the" being interlined between the forty third and forty fourth Lines of the second Page.

Attest WILLIAM JACKSON Secretary

of New Hampshire shall be entitled to chuse three, Massachusetts eight, Rhode-Island and Providence Plantations one, Connecticut five, New-York six, New Jersey four, Pennsylvania eight, Delaware one, Maryland six, Virginia ten, North Carolina five, South Carolina five, and Georgia three.

When vacancies happen in the Representation from any State, the Executive Authority thereof shall issue Writs of Election to fill such Vacancies.

The House of Representatives shall chuse their Speaker and other Officers; and shall have the sole Power of Impeachment.

SECTION 3

The Senate of the United States shall be composed of two Senators from each State, chosen by the Legislature thereof, for six Years; and each Senator shall have one Vote.

Immediately after they shall be assembled in Consequence of the first Election, they shall be divided as equally as may be into three Classes. The Seats of the Senators of the first Class shall be vacated at the Expiration of the second Year, of the second Class at the Expiration of the fourth Year, and of the third Class at the Expiration of the sixth Year, so that one third may be chosen every second Year; and if Vacancies happen by Resignation, or otherwise, during the Recess of the Legislature of any State, the Executive thereof may make temporary Appointments until the next Meeting of the Legislature, which shall then fill such Vacancies.

No Person shall be a Senator who shall not have attained to the Age of thirty Years, and been nine Years a Citizen of the United States, and who shall not, when elected, be an Inhabitant of that State for which he shall be chosen.

The Vice President of the United States shall be President of the Senate, but shall have no Vote, unless they be equally divided.

The Senate shall chuse their other Officers, and also a President pro tempore, in the Absence of the Vice President, or when he shall exercise the Office of President of the United States.

The Senate shall have the sole Power to try all Impeachments. When sitting for that Purpose, they shall be on Oath or Affirmation. When the President of the United States [is tried,] the Chief Justice shall preside: And no Person shall be convicted without the Concurrence of two thirds of the Members present.

Judgment in Cases of Impeachment shall not extend further than to removal from Office, and disqualification to hold and enjoy any Office of honor, Trust or Profit under the United States: but the Party convicted shall nevertheless be liable and subject to Indictment, Trial, Judgment and Punishment, according to Law.

SECTION 4

The Times, Places and Manner of holding Elections for Senators and Representatives, shall be prescribed in each State by the Legislature thereof; but the Congress may at any time by Law make or alter such Regulations, except as to the Places of chusing Senators.

The Congress shall assemble at least once in every Year, and such Meeting shall be on the first Monday in December, unless they shall by Law appoint a different Day.

SECTION 5

Each House shall be the Judge of the Elections, Returns and Qualifications of its own Members, and a Majority of each shall constitute a Quorum to do Business; but a smaller Number may adjourn from day to day, and may be authorized to compel the Attendance of absent Members, in such Manner, and under such Penalties as each House may provide.

Each House may determine the Rules of its Proceedings, punish its Members for disorderly Behaviour, and, with the Concurrence of two thirds, expel a Member.

Each House shall keep a Journal of its Proceedings, and from time to time publish the same, excepting such Parts as may in their Judgment require Secrecy; and the Yeas and Nays of the Members of either House on any question shall, at the Desire of one fifth of those Present, be entered on the Journal.

Neither House, during the Session of Congress, shall, without the Consent of the other, adjourn for more than three days, nor to any other Place than that in which the two Houses shall be sitting.

SECTION 6

The Senators and Representatives shall receive a Compensation for their Services, to be ascertained by Law, and paid out of the Treasury of the United States. They shall in all Cases, except Treason, Felony and Breach of the Peace, be privileged from Arrest during their attendance at the Session of their respective Houses, and in going to and returning from the same; and for any Speech or Debate in either House, they shall not be questioned in any other Place.

No Senator or Representative shall, during the Time for which he was elected, be appointed to any civil Office under the Authority of the United States, which shall have been created, or the Emoluments whereof shall have been encreased during such time; and no Person holding any Office under the United States, shall be a Member of either House during his Continuance in Office.

SECTION 7

All Bills for raising Revenue shall originate in the House of Representatives; but the Senate may propose or concur with Amendments as on other Bills.

Every Bill which shall have passed the House of Representatives and the Senate, shall, before it become a Law, be presented to the President of the United States; If he approve he shall sign it, but if not he shall return it, with his Objections to that House in which it shall have originated, who shall enter the Objections at large on their Journal, and proceed to reconsider it. If after such Reconsideration two thirds of that House shall agree to pass the Bill, it shall be sent, together with the Objections, to the other House, by which it shall likewise be reconsidered, and if approved by two thirds of that House, it shall become a Law. But in all such Cases the Votes of both Houses shall be determined by yeas and Nays, and the Names of the Persons voting for and against the Bill shall be entered on the Journal of each House respectively. If any Bill shall not be returned by the President within ten Days (Sundays excepted) after it shall have been presented to him, the Same shall be a Law, in like Manner as if he had signed it, unless the Congress by their Adjournment prevent its Return, in which Case it shall not be a Law.

Every Order, Resolution, or Vote to which the Concurrence of the Senate and House of Representatives may be necessary (except on a question of Adjournment) shall be presented to the President of the United States; and before the Same shall take Effect, shall be approved by him, or being disapproved by him, shall be repassed by two thirds of the Senate and House of Representatives, according to the Rules and Limitations prescribed in the Case of a Bill.

SECTION 8

The Congress shall have Power To lay and collect Taxes, Duties, Imposts and Excises, to pay the Debts and provide for the common Defence and general Welfare of the United States; but all Duties, Imposts and Excises shall be uniform throughout the United States;

To borrow Money on the credit of the United States;

To regulate Commerce with foreign Nations, and among the several States, and with the Indian Tribes;

To establish an uniform Rule of Naturalization, and uniform Laws on the subject of Bankruptcies throughout the United States;

To coin Money, regulate the Value thereof, and of foreign Coin, and fix the Standard of Weights and Measures;

To provide for the Punishment of counterfeiting the Securities and current Coin of the United States;

To establish Post Offices and post Roads;

To promote the Progress of Science and useful Arts, by securing for limited Times to Authors and Inventors the exclusive Right to their respective Writings and Discoveries;

To constitute Tribunals inferior to the supreme Court;

To define and punish Piracies and Felonies committed on the high Seas, and Offences against the Law of Nations;

To declare War, grant Letters of Marque and Reprisal, and make Rules concerning Captures on Land and Water;

To raise and support Armies, but no Appropriation of Money to that Use shall be for a longer Term than two Years;

To provide and maintain a Navy;

To make Rules for the Government and Regulation of the land and naval Forces;

To provide for calling forth the Militia to execute the Laws of the Union, suppress Insurrections and repel Invasions;

To provide for organizing, arming, and disciplining, the Militia, and for governing such Part of them as may be employed in the Service of the United States, reserving to the States respectively, the Appointment of the Officers, and the Authority of training the Militia according to the discipline prescribed by Congress;

To exercise exclusive Legislation in all Cases whatsoever, over such District (not exceeding ten Miles square) as may, by Cession of particular States, and the Acceptance of Congress, become the Seat of the

Government of the United States, and to exercise like Authority over all Places purchased by the Consent of the Legislature of the State in which the Same shall be, for the Erection of Forts, Magazines, Arsenals, dock-Yards, and other needful Buildings;—And

To make all Laws which shall be necessary and proper for carrying into Execution the foregoing Powers, and all other Powers vested by this Constitution in the Government of the United States, or in any Department or Officer thereof.

SECTION 9

The Migration or Importation of such Persons as any of the States now existing shall think proper to admit, shall not be prohibited by the Congress prior to the Year one thousand eight hundred and eight, but a Tax or duty may be imposed on such Importation, not exceeding ten dollars for each Person.

The Privilege of the Writ of Habeas Corpus shall not be suspended, unless when in Cases of Rebellion or Invasion the public Safety may require it.

No Bill of Attainder or ex post facto Law shall be passed.

No Capitation, or other direct, Tax shall be laid, unless in Proportion to the Census or Enumeration herein before directed to be taken.

No Tax or Duty shall be laid on Articles exported from any State.

No Preference shall be given by any Regulation of Commerce or Revenue to the Ports of one State over those of another: nor shall Vessels bound to, or from, one State, be obliged to enter, clear, or pay Duties in another.

No Money shall be drawn from the Treasury, but in Consequence of Appropriations made by Law; and a regular Statement and Account of the Receipts and Expenditures of all public Money shall be published from time to time.

No Title of Nobility shall be granted by the United States: And no Person holding any Office of Profit or Trust under them, shall, without the Consent of the Congress, accept of any present, Emolument, Office, or Title, of any kind whatever, from any King, Prince, or foreign State.

SECTION 10

No State shall enter into any Treaty, Alliance, or Confederation; grant Letters of Marque and Reprisal; coin Money; emit Bills of Credit;

make any Thing but gold and silver Coin a Tender in Payment of Debts; pass any Bill of Attainder, ex post facto Law, or Law impairing the Obligation of Contracts, or grant any Title of Nobility.

No State shall, without the Consent of [the] Congress, lay any Imposts or Duties on Imports or Exports, except what may be absolutely necessary for executing it's inspection Laws: and the net Produce of all Deputies and Imposts, laid by any State on Imports or Exports, shall be for the Use of the Treasury of the United States; and all such Laws shall be subject to the Revision and Controul of [the] Congress.

No State shall, without the Consent of Congress, lay any Duty of Tonnage, keep Troops, or Ships of War in time of Peace, enter into any Agreement or Compact with another State, or with a foreign Power, or engage in War, unless actually invaded, or in such imminent Danger as will not admit of delay.

ARTICLE II

SECTION 1

The executive Power shall be vested in a President of the United States of America. He shall hold his Office during the Term of four Years, and, together with the Vice President, chosen for the same Term, be elected, as follows

Each State shall appoint, in such Manner as the Legislature thereof may direct, a Number of Electors, equal to the whole Number of Senators and Representatives to which the State may be entitled in the Congress: but no Senator or Representative, or Person holding an Office of Trust or Profit under the United States, shall be appointed an Elector.

The Electors shall meet in their respective States, and vote by Ballot for two Persons, of whom one at least shall not be an Inhabitant of the same State with themselves. And they shall make a List of all the Persons voted for, and of the Number of Votes for each; which List they shall sign and certify, and transmit sealed to the Seat of the Government of the United States, directed to the President of the Senate. The President of the Senate shall, in the Presence of the Senate and House of Representatives, open all the Certificates, and the Votes shall then be counted. The Person having the greatest Number of Votes shall be the President, if such Number be a Majority of the whole Number of Electors appointed; and if there be more than one who have such Majority, and have an equal Number of Votes, then the House of Representatives shall immediately chuse by Ballot one of them for President; and if no Person have a Majority, then from the five highest on the List the said House shall in like Manner chuse the President. But in chusing the President, the Votes shall be taken by States, the Representation from each State having one Vote; A quorum for this Purpose shall consist of a Member or Members from two thirds of the States, and a Majority of all the States shall be necessary to a Choice. In every Case, after the Choice of the President, the Person having the greatest Number of Votes of the Electors shall be the Vice President. But if there should remain two or more who have equal Votes, the Senate shall chuse from them by Ballot the Vice President.

The Congress may determine the Time of chusing the Electors, and the Day on which they shall give their Votes; which Day shall be the same throughout the United States.

No Person except a natural born Citizen, or a Citizen of the United States, at the time of the Adoption of this Constitution, shall be eligible to the Office of President; neither shall any Person be eligible to that Office who shall not have attained to the Age of thirty five Years, and been fourteen Years a Resident within the United States.

In Case of the Removal of the President from Office, or of his Death, Resignation, or Inability to discharge the Powers and Duties of the said Office, the Same shall devolve on the Vice President, and the Congress may by Law provide for the Case of Removal, Death, Resignation or Inability, both of the President and Vice President, declaring what Officer shall then act as President, and such Officer shall act accordingly, until the Disability be removed, or a President shall be elected.

The President shall, at stated Times, receive for his Services, a Compensation, which shall neither be encreased nor diminished during the Period for which he shall have been elected, and he shall not receive within that Period any other Emolument from the United States, or any of them.

Before he enter on the Execution of his Office, he shall take the following Oath or Affirmation:—"I do solemnly swear (or affirm) that I will faithfully execute the Office of President of the United States, and will to the best of my Ability, preserve, protect and defend the Constitution of the United States."

SECTION 2

The President shall be Commander in Chief of the Army and Navy of the United States, and of the Militia of the several States, when called into the actual Service of the United States; he may require the Opinion, in writing, of the principal Officer in each of the executive Departments, upon any Subject relating to the Duties of their respective Offices, and he shall have Power to grant Reprieves and Pardons for Offences against the United States, except in Cases of Impeachment.

He shall have Power, by and with the Advice and Consent of the Senate, to make Treaties, provided two thirds of the Senators present concur; and he shall nominate, and by and with the Advice and Consent of the Senate, shall appoint Ambassadors, other public Ministers and Consuls, Judges of the supreme Court, and all other Officers of the United States, whose Appointments are not herein otherwise provided for, and which shall be established by Law: but the Congress may by Law vest the Appointment of such inferior Officers, as they think proper, in the President alone, in the Courts of Law, or in the Heads of Departments.

The President shall have Power to fill up all Vacancies that may happen during the Recess of the Senate, by granting Commissions which shall expire at the End of their next Session.

SECTION 3

He shall from time to time give to the Congress Information of the State of the Union, and recommend to their Consideration such Measures as he shall judge necessary and expedient; he may, on extraordinary Occasions, convene both Houses, or either of them, and in Case of Disagreement between them, with Respect to the Time of Adjournment, he may adjourn them to such Time as he shall think proper; he shall receive Ambassadors and other public Ministers; he shall take Care that the Laws be faithfully executed, and shall Commission all the Officers of the United States.

SECTION 4

The President, Vice President and all civil Officers of the United States, shall be removed from Office on Impeachment for, and Conviction of, Treason, Bribery, or other high Crimes and Misdemeanors.

ARTICLE III

SECTION 1

The judicial Power of the United States, shall be vested in one supreme Court, and in such inferior Courts as the Congress may from time to time ordain and establish. The Judges, both of the supreme and inferior Courts, shall hold their Offices during good Behaviour, and shall, at stated Times, receive for their Services, a Compensation, which shall not be diminished during their Continuance in Office.

SECTION 2

The judicial Power shall extend to all Cases, in Law and Equity, arising under this Constitution, the Laws of the United States, and Treaties made, or which shall be made, under their Authority;—to all Cases affecting Ambassadors, other public Ministers and Consuls;—to all Cases of admiralty and maritime Jurisdiction;—to Controversies to which the United States shall be a Party;—to Controversies between two or more States;—between a State and Citizens of another State;—between Citizens of different States,—between Citizens of the same State claiming Lands under Grants of different States, and between a State, or the Citizens thereof, and foreign States, Citizens or Subjects.

In all Cases affecting Ambassadors, other public Ministers and Consuls, and those in which a State shall be Party, the supreme Court shall have original Jurisdiction. In all the other Cases before mentioned, the supreme Court shall have appellate Jurisdiction, both as to Law and Fact, with such Exceptions, and under such Regulations as the Congress shall make.

The Trial of all Crimes, except in Cases of Impeachment, shall be by Jury; and such Trial shall be held in the State where the said Crimes shall have been committed, but when not committed within any State, the Trial shall be at such Place or Places as the Congress may by Law have directed.

SECTION 3

Treason against the United States, shall consist only in levying War against them, or in adhering to their Enemies, giving them Aid and Comfort. No Person shall be convicted of Treason unless on the Testimony of two Witnesses to the same overt Act, or on Confession in open Court.

The Congress shall have Power to declare the Punishment of Treason, but no Attainder of Treason shall work Corruption of Blood, or Forfeiture except during the Life of the Person attainted.

ARTICLE IV

SECTION 1

Full Faith and Credit shall be given in each State to the public Acts, Records, and judicial Proceedings of every other State. And the Congress may by general Laws prescribe the Manner in which such Acts, Records and Proceedings shall be proved, and the Effect thereof.

SECTION 2

The Citizens of each State shall be entitled to all Privileges and Immunities of Citizens in the several States.

A Person charged in any State with Treason, Felony, or other Crime, who shall flee from Justice, and be found in another State, shall on Demand of the executive Authority of the State from which he fled, be delivered up, to be removed to the State having Jurisdiction of the Crime.

No Person held to Service or Labour in one State, under the Laws thereof, escaping into another, shall, in Consequence of any Law or Regulation therein, be discharged from such Service or Labour, but shall be delivered up on Claim of the Party to whom such Service or Labour may be due.

SECTION 3

New States may be admitted by the Congress into this Union; but no new State shall be formed or erected within the Jurisdiction of any other State; nor any State be formed by the Junction of two or more States, or Parts of States, without the Consent of the Legislatures of the States concerned as well as of the Congress.

The Congress shall have Power to dispose of and make all needful Rules and Regulations respecting the Territory or other Property belonging to the United States; and nothing in this Constitution shall be so construed as to Prejudice any Claims of the United States, or of any particular State.

SECTION 4

The United States shall guarantee to every State in this Union a Republican Form of Government, and shall protect each of them against Invasion; and on Application of the Legislature, or of the Executive (when the Legislature cannot be convened) against domestic Violence.

ARTICLE V

The Congress, whenever two thirds of both Houses shall deem it necessary, shall propose Amendments to this Constitution, or, on the Application of the Legislatures of two thirds of the several States, shall call a Convention for proposing Amendments, which, in either Case, shall be valid to all Intents and Purposes, as Part of this Constitution, when ratified by the Legislatures of three fourths of the several States, or by Conventions in three fourths thereof, as the one or the other Mode of Ratification may be proposed by the Congress; Provided that no Amendment which may be made prior to the Year One thousand eight hundred and eight shall in any Manner affect the first and fourth Clauses in the Ninth Section of the first Article; and that no State, without its Consent, shall be deprived of it's equal Suffrage in the Senate.

ARTICLE VI

All Debts contracted and Engagements entered into, before the Adoption of this Constitution, shall be as valid against the United States under this Constitution, as under the Confederation.

This Constitution, and the Laws of the United States which shall be made in Pursuance thereof; and all Treaties made, or which shall be made, under the Authority of the United States, shall be the supreme Law of the Land; and the Judges in every State shall be bound thereby, any Thing in the Constitution or Laws of any State to the Contrary notwithstanding.

The Senators and Representatives before mentioned, and the Members of the several State Legislatures, and all executive and judicial Officers, both of the United States and of the several States, shall be bound by Oath or Affirmation, to support this Constitution; but no religious Test shall ever be required as a Qualification to any Office or public Trust under the United States.

ARTICLE VII

The Ratification of the Conventions of nine States, shall be sufficient for the Establishment of this Constitution between the States so ratifying the Same.

done in Convention by the Unanimous Consent of the States present the Seventeenth Day of September in the Year of our Lord one thousand seven hundred and Eighty seven and of the Independance of the United States of America the Twelfth. In witness whereof We have hereunto subscribed our Names,

G° WASHINGTON—Presd[t]
and deputy from Virginia

DELAWARE
Geo: Read
Gunning Bedford jun
John Dickinson
Richard Bassett
Jaco: Broom

MARYLAND
James M[c]Henry
Dan of S[t] Tho[s] Jenifer
Dan[l] Carroll

VIRGINIA
John Blair—
James Madison Jr.

NORTH CAROLINA
W[m] Blount
Rich[d] Dobbs Spaight.
Hu Williamson

SOUTH CAROLINA
J. Rutledge
Charles Cotesworth Pinckney
Charles Pinckney
Pierce Butler.

GEORGIA
William Few
Abr Baldwin

NEW HAMPSHIRE
John Langdon
Nicholas Gilman

MASSACHUSETTS
Nathaniel Gorham
Rufus King

CONNECTICUT
W[m] Sam[l] Johnson
Roger Sherman

NEW YORK
Alexander Hamilton

NEW JERSEY
Wil: Livingston
David Brearley.
W[m] Paterson.
Jona: Dayton

PENSYLVANIA
B Franklin
Thomas Mifflin
Rob[t] Morris
Geo. Clymer
Tho[s] FitzSimons
Jared Ingersoll
James Wilson
Gouv Morris

[AMENDMENT I]

Congress shall make no law respecting an establishment of religion, or prohibiting the free exercise thereof; or abridging the freedom of speech, or of the press; or the right of the people peaceably to assemble, and to petition the Government for a redress of grievances.

[AMENDMENT II]

A well regulated Militia, being necessary to the security of a free State, the right of the people to keep and bear Arms, shall not be infringed.

[AMENDMENT III]

No Soldier shall, in time of peace be quartered in any house, without the consent of the Owner, nor in time of war, but in a manner to be prescribed by law.

[AMENDMENT IV]

The right of the people to be secure in their persons, houses, papers, and effects, against unreasonable searches and seizures, shall not be violated, and no Warrants shall issue, but upon probable cause, supported by Oath or affirmation, and particularly describing the place to be searched, and the persons or things to be seized.

[AMENDMENT V]

No person shall be held to answer for a capital, or otherwise infamous crime, unless on a presentment or indictment of a Grand Jury, except in cases arising in the land or naval forces, or in the Militia, when in actual service in time of War or public danger; nor shall any person be subject for the same offense to be twice put in jeopardy of life or limb, nor shall be compelled in any criminal case to be a witness against himself, nor be deprived of life, liberty, or property, without due process of law; nor shall private property be taken for public use, without just compensation.

[AMENDMENT VI]

In all criminal prosecutions, the accused shall enjoy the right to a speedy and public trial, by an impartial jury of the State and district wherein the crime shall have been committed, which district shall have been previously ascertained by law, and to be informed of the nature and cause of the accusation; to be confronted with the witnesses against him; to have compulsory process for obtaining Witnesses in his favor, and to have the Assistance of Counsel for his defence.

[AMENDMENT VII]

In Suits at common law, where the value in controversy shall exceed twenty dollars, the right of trial by jury shall be preserved, and no fact tried by a jury, shall be otherwise re-examined in any Court of the United States, than according to the rules of the common law.

[AMENDMENT VIII]

Excessive bail shall not be required, nor excessive fines imposed, nor cruel and unusual punishments inflicted.

[AMENDMENT IX]

The enumeration in the Constitution, of certain rights, shall not be construed to deny or disparage others retained by the people.

[AMENDMENT X]

The powers not delegated to the United States by the Constitution, nor prohibited by it to the States, are reserved to the States respectively, or to the people.

[AMENDMENT XI]

The Judicial power of the United States shall not be construed to extend to any suit in law or equity, commenced or prosecuted against one of the United States by Citizens of another State, or by Citizens or Subjects of any Foreign State.

[AMENDMENT XII]

The Electors shall meet in their respective states, and vote by ballot for President and Vice-President, one of whom, at least, shall not be an inhabitant of the same state with themselves; they shall name in their ballots the person voted for as President, and in distinct ballots the person voted for as Vice-President, and they shall make distinct lists of all persons voted for as President, and of all persons voted for as Vice-President, and of the number of votes for each, which lists they shall sign and certify, and transmit sealed to the seat of the government of the United States, directed to the President of the Senate;—The President of the Senate shall, in the presence of the Senate and House of Representatives, open all the certificates and the votes shall then be counted;—The person having the greatest number of votes for President, shall be the President, if such number be a majority of the whole number of Electors appointed; and if no person have such majority, then from the persons having the highest numbers not exceeding three on the list of those voted for as President, the House of Representatives shall choose immediately, by ballot, the President. But in choosing the President, the votes shall be taken by states, the representation from each state having one vote; a quorum for this purpose shall consist of a member or members from two-thirds of the states, and a majority of all the states shall be necessary to a choice. And if the House of Representatives shall not choose a President whenever the right of choice shall devolve upon them, before the fourth day of March next following, then the Vice-President shall act as President, as in the case of the death or other constitutional disability of the President.—The person having the greatest number of votes as Vice-President, shall be the Vice-President, if such number be a majority of the whole number of Electors appointed, and if no person have a majority, then from the two highest numbers on the list, the Senate shall choose the Vice-President; a quorum for the purpose shall consist of two-thirds of the whole number of Senators, and a majority of the whole number shall be necessary to a choice. But no person constitutionally ineligible to the office of President shall be eligible to that of Vice-President of the United States.

[AMENDMENT XIII]

SECTION 1. Neither slavery nor involuntary servitude, except as a punishment for crime whereof the party shall have been duly convicted, shall exist within the United States, or any place subject to their jurisdiction.

SECTION 2. Congress shall have power to enforce this article by appropriate legislation.

[AMENDMENT XIV]

SECTION 1. All persons born or naturalized in the United States, and subject to the jurisdiction thereof, are citizens of the United

States and of the State wherein they reside. No State shall make or enforce any law which shall abridge the privileges or immunities of citizens of the United States; nor shall any State deprive any person of life, liberty, or property, without due process of law; nor deny to any person within its jurisdiction the equal protection of the laws.

SECTION 2. Representatives shall be apportioned among the several States according to their respective numbers, counting the whole number of persons in each State, excluding Indians not taxed. But when the right to vote at any election for the choice of electors for President and Vice President of the United States, Representatives in Congress, the Executive and Judicial officers of a State, or the members of the Legislature thereof, is denied to any of the male inhabitants of such State, being twenty-one years of age, and citizens of the United States, or in any way abridged, except for participation in rebellion, or other crime, the basis of representation therein shall be reduced in the proportion which the number of such male citizens shall bear to the whole number of male citizens twenty-one years of age in such State.

SECTION 3. No person shall be a Senator or Representative in Congress, or elector of President and Vice President, or hold any office, civil or military, under the United States, or under any State, who, having previously taken an oath, as a member of Congress, or as an officer of the United States, or as a member of any State legislature, or as an executive or judicial officer of any State, to support the Constitution of the United States, shall have engaged in insurrection or rebellion against the same, or given aid or comfort to the enemies thereof. But Congress may by a vote of two-thirds of each House, remove such disability.

SECTION 4. The validity of the public debt of the United States, authorized by law, including debts incurred for payment of pensions and bounties for services in suppressing insurrection or rebellion, shall not be questioned. But neither the United States nor any State shall assume or pay any debt or obligation incurred in aid of insurrection or rebellion against the United States, or any claim for the loss or emancipation of any slave; but all such debts, obligations and claims shall be held illegal and void.

SECTION 5. The Congress shall have power to enforce, by appropirate legislation, the provisions of this article.

[AMENDMENT XV]

SECTION 1. The right of citizens of the United States to vote shall not be denied or abridged by the United States or by any State on account of race, color, or previous condition of servitude.——

SECTION 2. The Congress shall have power to enforce this article by appropriate legislation.——

[AMENDMENT XVI]

The Congress shall have power to lay and collect taxes on incomes, from whatever source derived, without apportionment among the several States, and without regard to any census or enumeration.

[AMENDMENT XVII]

The Senate of the United States shall be composed of two Senators from each State, elected by the people thereof, for six years; and each Senator shall have one vote. The electors in each State shall have the qualifications requisite for electors of the most numerous branch of the State legislatures.

When vacancies happen in the representation of any State in the Senate, the executive authority of such State shall issue writs of election to fill such vacancies: *Provided*, That the legislature of any State may empower the executive thereof to make temporary appointments until the people fill the vacancies by election as the legislature may direct.

This amendment shall not be so construed as to affect the election or term of any Senator chosen before it becomes valid as part of the Constitution.

[AMENDMENT XVIII]

SECTION 1. After one year from the ratification of this article the manufacture, sale, or transportation of intoxicating liquors within, the importation thereof into, or the exportation thereof from the United States and all territory subject to the jurisdiction thereof for beverage purposes is hereby prohibited.

SECTION 2. The Congress and the several States shall have concurrent power to enforce this article by appropriate legislation.

SECTION 3. This article shall be inoperative unless it shall have been ratified as an amendment to the Constitution by the legislatures of the several States, as provided in the Constitution, within seven years from the date of the submission hereof to the States by the Congress.

[AMENDMENT XIX]

The right of citizens of the United States to vote shall not be denied or abridged by the United States or by any State on account of sex.

Congress shall have power to enforce this article by appropriate legislation.

[AMENDMENT XX]

SECTION 1. The terms of the President and Vice President shall end at noon on the 20th day of January, and the terms of Senators and Representatives at noon on the 3d day of January, of the years in which such terms would have ended if this article had not been ratified; and the terms of their successors shall then begin.

SECTION 2. The Congress shall assemble at least once in every year, and such meeting shall be at noon on the 3d day of January, unless they shall by law appoint a different day.

SECTION 3. If, at the time fixed for the beginning of the term of the President, the President elect shall have died, the Vice President elect shall become President. If a President shall not have been chosen before the time fixed for the beginning of his term, or if the President elect shall have failed to qualify, then the Vice President elect shall act as President until a President shall have qualified; and the Congress may by law provide for the case wherein neither a President elect nor a Vice President elect shall have qualified, declaring who shall then act as President, or the manner in which one who is to act shall be selected, and such person shall act accordingly until a President or Vice President shall have qualified.

SECTION 4. The Congress may by law provide for the case of the death of any of the persons from whom the House of Representatives may choose a President whenever the right of choice shall have devolved upon them, and for the case of the death of any of the persons from whom the Senate may choose a Vice President whenever the right of choice shall have devolved upon them.

SECTION 5. Sections 1 and 2 shall take effect on the 15th day of October following the ratification of this article.

SECTION 6. This article shall be inoperative unless it shall have been ratified as an amendment to the Constitution by the legislatures of three-fourths of the several States within seven years from the date of its submission.

[AMENDMENT XXI]

SECTION 1. The eighteenth article of amendment to the Constitution of the United States is hereby repealed.

SECTION 2. The transportation or importation into any State, Territory, or possession of the United States for delivery or use therein of intoxicating liquors, in violation of the laws thereof, is hereby prohibited.

SECTION 3. This article shall be inoperative unless it shall have been ratified as an amendment to the Constitution by conventions in the several States, as provided in the Constitution, within seven years from the date of the submission hereof to the States by the Congress.

[AMENDMENT XXII]

SECTION 1. No person shall be elected to the office of the President more than twice, and no person who has held the office of President, or acted as President, for more than two years of a term to which some other person was elected President shall be elected to the office of the President more than once. But this Article shall not apply to any person holding the office of President when this Article was proposed by the Congress, and shall not prevent any person who may be holding the office of President, or acting as President, during the term within which this Article becomes operative from holding the office of President or acting as President during the remainder of such term.

SECTION 2. This article shall be inoperative unless it shall have been ratified as an amendment to the Constitution by the legislatures of three-fourths of the several States within seven years from the date of its submission to the States by the Congress.

[AMENDMENT XXIII]

SECTION 1. The District constituting the seat of Government of the United States shall appoint in such manner as the Congress may direct:

A number of electors of President and Vice President equal to the whole number of Senators and Representatives in Congress to which the District would be entitled if it were a State, but in no event more than the least populous State; they shall be in addition to those appointed by the States, but they shall be considered, for the purposes of the election of President and Vice President, to be electors appointed by a State; and they shall meet in the District and perform such duties as provided by the twelfth article of amendment.

SECTION 2. The Congress shall have power to enforce this article by appropriate legislation.

[AMENDMENT XXIV]

SECTION 1. The right of citizens of the United States to vote in any primary or other election for President or Vice President, for electors for President or Vice President, or for Senator or Representative in Congress, shall not be denied or abridged by the United States or any State by reason of failure to pay any poll tax or other tax.

SECTION 2. The Congress shall have power to enforce this article by appropriate legislation.

[AMENDMENT XXV]

SECTION 1. In case of the removal of the President from office or of his death or resignation, the Vice President shall become President.

SECTION 2. Whenever there is a vacancy in the office of the Vice President, the President shall nominate a Vice President who shall take office upon confirmation by a majority vote of both Houses of Congress.

SECTION 3. Whenever the President transmits to the President pro tempore of the Senate and the Speaker of the House of Representatives his written declaration that he is unable to discharge the powers and duties of his office, and until he transmits to them a written declaration to the contrary, such powers and duties shall be discharged by the Vice President as Acting President.

SECTION 4. Whenever the Vice President and a majority of either the principal officers of the executive departments or of such other body as Congress may by law provide, transmit to the President pro tempore of the Senate and the Speaker of the House of Representatives their written declaration that the President is unable to discharge the powers and duties of his office, the Vice President shall immediately assume the powers and duties of the office as Acting President.

Thereafter, when the President transmits to the President pro tempore of the Senate and the Speaker of the House of Representatives his written declaration that no inability exists, he shall resume the powers and duties of his office unless the Vice President and a majority of either the principal officers of the executive department or of such other body as Congress may by law provide, transmit within four days to the President pro tempore of the Senate and the Speaker of the House of Representatives their written declaration that the President is unable to discharge the powers and duties of his office. Thereupon Congress shall decide the issue, assembling within forty-eight hours for that purpose if not in session. If the Congress, within twenty-one days after the receipt of the latter written declaration, or, if Congress is not in session, within twenty-one days after Congress is required to assemble, determines by two-thirds vote of both Houses that the President is unable to discharge the powers and duties of his office, the Vice President shall continue to discharge the same as Acting President; otherwise, the President shall resume the powers and duties of his office.

GEORGE WASHINGTON'S FAREWELL ADDRESS TO THE PEOPLE OF THE UNITED STATES

Friends, & Fellow-Citizens

The period for a new election of a Citizen, to administer the Executive government of the United States, being not far distant, and the time actually arrived, when your thoughts must be employed in designating the person, who is to be cloathed with that important trust, it appears to me proper, especially as it may conduce to a more distinct expression of the public voice, that I should now apprise you of the resolution I have formed, to decline being considered among the number of those, out of whom a choice is to be made.—

I beg you, at the same time, to do me the justice to be assured, that this resolution has not been taken, without a strict regard to all the considerations appertaining to the relation, which binds a dutiful citizen to his country—and that, in withdrawing the tender of service which silence in my situation might imply, I am influenced by no diminution of zeal for your future interest, no deficiency of grateful respect for your past kindness; but am supported by a full conviction that the step is compatible with both.

The acceptance of, & continuance hitherto in, the office to which your suffrages have twice called me, have been a uniform sacrifice of inclination to the opinion of duty, and to a deference for what appeared to be your desire.—I constantly hoped, that it would have been much earlier in my power, consistently with motives, which I was not at liberty to disregard, to return to that retirement, from which I had been reluctantly drawn.—The strength of my inclination to do this, previous to the last election, had even led to the preparation of an address to declare it to you; but mature reflection on the then perplexed & critical posture of our affairs with foreign Nations, and the unanimous advice of persons entitled to my confidence, impelled me to abandon the idea.—

I rejoice, that the state of your concerns, external as well as internal, no longer renders the pursuit of inclination incompatible with the sentiment of duty, or propriety; & am persuaded whatever partiality may be retained for my services, that in the present circumstances of our country, you will not disapprove my determination to retire.—

The impressions, with which, I first undertook the arduous trust, were explained on the proper occasion.—In the discharge of this trust,

I will only say, that I have, with good intentions, contributed towards the organization and administration of the government, the best exertions of which a very fallible judgment was capable.—Not unconscious in the outset, of the inferiority of my qualifications, experience in my own eyes, perhaps still more in the eyes of others, has strengthned the motives to diffidence of myself; and every day the encreasing weight of years admonishes me more and more, that the shade of retirement is as necessary to me as it will be welcome.—Satisfied that if any circumstances have given peculiar value to my services, they were temporary, I have the consolation to believe, that while choice and prudence invite me to quit the political scene, patriotism does not forbid it.—

In looking forward to the moment, which is intended to terminate the career of my public life, my feelings do not permit me to suspend the deep acknowledgment of that debt of gratitude which I owe to my beloved country,—for the many honors it has conferred upon me; still more for the stedfast confidence with which it has supported me; and for the opportunities I have thence enjoyed of manifesting my inviolable attachment, by services faithful & persevering, though in usefulness unequal to my zeal.—If benefits have resulted to our country from these services, let it always be remembered to your praise, and as an instructive example in our annals, that under circumstances in which the Passions agitated in every direction were liable to mislead, amidst appearances sometimes dubious,—viscissitudes of fortune often discouraging,—in situations in which not unfrequently want of success has countenanced the spirit of criticism,—the constancy of your support was the essential prop of the efforts, and a guarantee of the plans by which they were effected.—Profoundly penetrated with this idea, I shall carry it with me to my grave, as a strong incitement to unceasing vows that Heaven may continue to you the choicest tokens of its beneficence—that your union & brotherly affection may be perpetual—that the free constitution, which is the work of your hands, may be sacredly maintained—that its administration in every department may be stamped with wisdom and virtue—that, in fine, the happiness of the people of these States, under the auspices of liberty, may be made complete, by so careful a preservation and so prudent a use of this blessing as will acquire to them the glory of recommending it to the applause, the affection—and adoption of every nation which is yet a stranger to it.

Here, perhaps, I ought to stop. But a solicitude for your welfare, which cannot end but with my life, and the apprehension of danger, natural to that solicitude, urge me on an occasion like the present, to offer to your solemn contemplation, and to recommend to your frequent review, some sentiments; which are the result of much reflection, of no inconsiderable observation, and which appear to me all important to the permanency of your felicity as a People.—These will be offered to you with the more freedom, as you can only see in them the disinterested warnings of a parting friend, who can possibly have no personal motive to biass his counsel. Nor can I forget, as an encouragement to it, your indulgent reception of my sentiments on a former and not dissimilar occasion

Interwoven as is the love of liberty with every ligament of your hearts, no recommendation of mine is necessary to fortify or confirm the attachment.—

The Unity of Government which constitutes you one people is also now dear to you.—It is justly so;—for it is a main Pillar in the Edifice of your real independence, the support of your tranquility at home; your peace abroad; of your safety;—of your prosperity;—of that very Liberty which you so highly prize.—But as it is easy to foresee, that from different causes & from different quarters, much pains will be taken, many artifices employed, to weaken in your minds the conviction of this truth;—as this is the point in your political fortress against which the batteries of internal & external enemies will be most constantly and actively (though often covertly & insidiously) directed, it is of infinite moment, that you should properly estimate the immense value of your national union to your collective & individual happiness; —that you should cherish a cordial, habitual & immoveable attachment to it; accustoming yourself to think and speak of it as of the Palladium of your political safety and prosperity; watching for its preservation with jealous anxiety; discountenancing whatever may suggest even a suspicion that it can in any event be abandoned, and indignantly frowning upon the first dawning of every attempt to alienate any portion of our Country from the rest, or to enfeeble the sacred ties which now link together the various parts.

For this you have every inducement of sympathy and interest.—Citizens by birth or choice, of a common country, that country has a right to concentrate your affections.—The name of AMERICAN, which belongs to you, in your national capacity, must always exalt the just pride of Patriotism, more than any appellation derived from local discriminations.—With slight shades of difference, you have the same Religeon, Manners, Habits & political Principles.—You have in a common cause fought & triumphed together—The independence & liberty you possess are the work of joint councils, and joint efforts—of common dangers, sufferings and successes.—

But these considerations, however powerfully they address themselves to your sensibility are greatly outweighed by those which apply more immediately to your Interest.—Here every portion of our country finds the most commanding motives for carefully guarding & preserving the union of the whole.

The *North*, in an unrestrained intercourse with the *South*, protected by the equal Laws of a common government, finds in the productions of the latter, great additional resources of maratime & commercial enterprise—and precious materials of manufacturing industry.—The *South* in the same Intercourse, benefitting by the agency of the *North*, sees its agriculture grow & its commerce expand. Turning partly into its own channels the seamen of the *North*, it finds its particular navigation invigorated;—and while it contributes, in different ways, to nourish & increase the general mass of the national navigation, it looks forward to the protection of a maratime strength, to which itself is unequally adapted.—The *East*, in a like intercourse with the *West*, already finds, and in the progressive improvement of interior communications, by land & water, will more & more find a valuable vent for the commodities which it brings from abroad, or manufactures at home.—The *West* derives from the *East* supplies requisite to its growth and comfort,—and what is perhaps of still greater consequence, it must of necessity owe the *secure* enjoyment of indispensable *outlets* for its own productions to the weight, influence, and the future maritime strength of the Atlantic side of the Union, directed by an indissoluble community of Interest as *one Nation*.—Any other tenure by which the *West* can hold this essential advantage, whether derived from its own seperate strength, or from an apostate & unnatural connection with any foreign Power, must be intrinsically precarious;—

While then every part of our country thus feels an immediate & particular Interest in union, all the parts combined cannot fail to find in the united mass of means & efforts greater strength, greater resource, proportionably greater security from external danger, a less frequent interruption of their Peace by foreign Nations;—and, what is of inestimable value! they must derive from union an exemption from those broils and Wars between themselves, which so frequently afflict neighbouring countries, not tied together by the same government; which their own rivalships alone would be sufficient to produce, but which opposite foreign alliances, attachments & intriegues would stimulate and imbitter.—Hence likewise they will avoid the necessity of those overgrown military establishments, which under any form of Government are inauspicious to liberty, and which are to be regarded as particularly hostile to Republican Liberty: In this sense it is, that your union ought to be considered as a main prop of your liberty, and that the love of the one ought to endear to you the preservation of the other.—

These considerations speak a persuasive language to every reflecting & virtuous mind,—and exhibit the continuance of the UNION as a primary object of Patriotic desire.—Is there a doubt, whether a common government can embrace so large a sphere?—Let experience solve it.—To listen to mere speculation in such a case were criminal. —We are authorized to hope that a proper organization of the whole, with the auxiliary agency of governments for the respective Subdivisions, will afford a happy issue to the experiment.—'Tis well worth a fair and full experiment With such powerful and obvious motives to union, affecting all parts of our country, while experience shall not have demonstrated its impracticability, there will always be reason to distrust the patriotism of those, who in any quarter may endeavor to weaken its bands.—

In contemplating the causes which may disturb our Union, it occurs as matter of serious concern, that any ground should have been furnished for characterizing parties by *Geographical* discriminations—*Northern* and *Southern*—*Atlantic* and *Western*; whence designing men may endeavour to excite a belief that there is a real difference of local interests and views. One of the expedients of Party to acquire influence, within particular districts, is to misrepresent the opinions & aims of other Districts.—You cannot shield yourselves too much against the jealousies & heart burnings which spring from these misrepresentations.—They tend to render alien to each other those who ought to be bound together by fraternal affection.—The Inhabitants of our Western country have lately had a useful lesson on this head.—They have seen, in the Negociation by the Executive, and in the unanimous ratification by the Senate, of the Treaty with Spain, and in the universal satisfaction at that event, throughout the United States, a decisive proof how unfounded were the suspicions propagated among them of a policy in the General Government and in the Atlantic States unfriendly to their Interests in regard to the MISSISSIPPI—They have been witnesses to the formation of two Treaties, that with G: Britain, and that with Spain, which secure to them every thing they could desire, in respect to our Foreign relations, towards confirming their prosperity.—Will it not be their wisdom to rely for the preservation of these advantages on the UNION by which they were procured?—Will they not henceforth be deaf to those advisers, if such there are, who would sever them from their Brethren and connect them with Aliens?—

To the efficacy and permanency of Your Union, a Government for the whole is indispensable.—No alliances however strict between the parts can be an adequate substitute.—They must inevitably experience the infractions & interruptions which all alliances in all times have experienced.—Sensible of this momentous truth, you have improved upon your first essay, by the adoption of a Constitution of Government, better calculated than your former for an intimate Union, and for the efficacious management of your common concerns.—This government, the offspring of our own choice uninfluenced and unawed, adopted upon full investigation & mature deliberation, completely free in its principles, in the distribution of its powers, uniting security with energy, and containing within itself a provision for its own amendment, has a just claim to your confidence and your support.—Respect for its authority, compliance with its Laws, acquiescence in its measures, are duties enjoined by the fundamental maxims of true Liberty.—The basis of our political systems is the right of the people to make and to alter their Constitutions of Government.—But the Constitution which at any time exists, 'till changed by an explicit and authentic act of the whole People, is sacredly obligatory upon all.—The very idea of the power and the right of the People to establish Government presupposes the duty of every individual to obey the established Government.

All obstructions to the execution of the Laws, all combinations and associations, under whatever plausible character, with the real design to direct, controul counteract, or awe the regular deliberation and action of the constituted authorities are destructive of this fundamental principle and of fatal tendency.—They serve to organize faction, to give it an artificial and extraordinary force—to put in the place of the delegated will of the Nation, the will of a party;—often a small but artful and enterprising minority of the community;—and, according to the alternate triumphs of different parties, to make the public administration the mirror of the ill concerted and incongruous projects of faction, rather than the Organ of consistent and wholesome plans digested by common councils and modefied by mutual interests. —However combinations or associations of the above description may now & then answer popular ends, they are likely, in the course of time and things, to become potent engines, by which cunning, ambitious and unprincipled men will be enabled to subvert the Power of the People, & to usurp for themselves the reins of Government; destroying afterwards the very engines which have lifted them to unjust dominion.—

Towards the preservation of your Government and the permanency of your present happy state, it is requisite, not only that you steadily discountenance irregular oppositions to its acknowledged authority, but also that you resist with care the spirit of innovation upon its principles however specious the pretexts.—One method of assault may be to effect, in the forms of the Constitution, alterations which will impair the energy of the system, and thus to undermine what cannot be directly overthrown.—In all the changes to which you may be invited, remember that time and habit are at least as necessary to fix the true character of Governments, as of other human institutions—that experience is the surest standard, by which to test the real tendency of the existing Constitution of a country—that facility in changes upon the credit of mere hypotheses & opinion exposes to perpetual change, from the endless variety of hypotheses and opinion:—and remember, especially, that for the efficient management of your common interests, in a country so extensive as ours, a Government of as much vigour as is consistent with the perfect security of Liberty is indispensable—Liberty itself will find in such a Government, with powers properly distributed and adjusted, its surest Guardian.—It is indeed little else than a name, where the Government is too feeble to withstand the enterprises of faction, to confine each member of the Society within the limits prescribed by the laws & to maintain all in the secure & tranquil enjoyment of the rights of person & property.—

I have already intimated to you the danger of Parties in the State, with particular reference to the founding of them on Geographical discriminations.—Let me now take a more comprehensive view, & warn you in the most solemn manner against the baneful effects of the Spirit of Party, generally

This Spirit, unfortunately, is inseperable from our nature, having its root in the strongest passions of the human mind.—It exists under different shapes in all Governments, more or less stifled, controuled, or repressed; but in those of the popular form it is seen in its greatest rankness and is truly their worst enemy.—

The alternate domination of one faction over another, sharpened by the spirit of revenge natural to party dissention, which in different ages & countries has perpetrated the most horrid enormities, is itself a frightful despotism.—But this leads at length to a more formal and permanent despotism.—The disorders & miseries, which result, gradually incline the minds of men to seek security & repose in the absolute power of an Individual: and sooner or later the chief of some prevailing faction more able or more fortunate than his competitors, turns this disposition to the purposes of his own elevation, on the ruins of Public Liberty.—

Without looking forward to an extremity of this kind (which nevertheless ought not to be entirely out of sight) the common & continual mischiefs of the spirit of Party are sufficient to make it the interest and the duty of a wise People to discourage and restrain it.—

It serves always to distract the Public councils and enfeeble the Public administration.—It agitates the Community with ill founded jealousies and false alarms, kindles the animosity of one part against another, foments occasionally riot & insurrection.—It opens the doors to foreign influence & corruption, which find a facilitated access to the government itself through the channels of party passions. Thus the policy and the will of one country, are subjected to the policy and will of another.—

There is an opinion that parties in free countries are useful checks upon the administration of the Government and serve to keep alive the spirit of Liberty.—This within certain limits is probably true— and in Governments of a Monarchical cast Patriotism may look with endulgence, if not with favour, upon the spirit of party.—But in those of the popular character, in Governments purely elective, it is a spirit not to be encouraged.—From their natural tendency, it is certain there will always be enough of that spirit for every salutary purpose.— and there being constant danger of excess, the effort ought to be, by force of public opinion, to mitigate & assuage it.—A fire not to be quenched; it demands a uniform vigilance to prevent its bursting into a flame, lest instead of warming it should consume.—

It is important, likewise, that the habits of thinking in a free Country should inspire caution in those entrusted with its administration, to confine themselves within their respective Constitutional spheres; avoiding in the exercise of the Powers of one department to encroach upon another.—The spirit of encroachment tends to consolidate the powers of all the departments in one, and thus to create whatever the form of government, a real despotism.—A just estimate of that love of power, and proneness to abuse it, which predominates in the human heart, is sufficient to satisfy us of the truth of this position.—The necessity of reciprocal checks in the exercise of political power; by dividing and distributing it into different depositories, & constituting each the Guardian of the Public Weal against invasions by the others, has been evinced by experiments ancient & modern;—some of them in our country & under our own eyes.—To preserve them must be as necessary as to institute them.—If in the opinion of the People, the distribution or modification of the Constitutional powers be in any particular wrong, let it be corrected by an amendment in the way which the Constitution designates.—But let there be no change by usurpation; for though this, in one instance, may be the instrument of good, it is the customary weapon by which free governments are detroyed.—The precedent must always greatly overbalance in permanent evil any partial or transient benefit which the use can at any time yield.—

Of all the dispositions and habits which lead to political prosperity, Religion and morality are indispensable supports.—In vain would that man claim the tribute of Patriotism, who should labour to subvert these great Pillars of human happiness, these firmest props of the duties of Men & citizens.—The mere Politician, equally with the pious man ought to respect & to cherish them.—A volume could not trace all their connections with private & public felicity.—Let it simply be asked where is the security for property, for reputation, for life, if the sense of religious obligation *desert* the oaths, which are the instruments of investigation in Courts of Justice?—And let us with caution indulge the supposition, that morality can be maintained without religion.—Whatever may be conceded to the influence of refined education on minds of peculiar structure—reason & experience both forbid us to expect that national morality can prevail in exclusion of religious principle.—

'Tis substantially true, that virtue or morality is a necessary spring of popular government.—The rule indeed extends with more or less force to every species of Free Government.—Who that is a sincere friend to it, can look with indifference upon attempts to shake the foundation of the fabric

Promote then as an object of primary importance, Institutions for the general diffusion of knowledge.—In proportion as the structure of a government gives force to public opinion, it is essential that public opinion should be enlightened

As a very important source of strength & security, cherish public credit.—One method of preserving it is to use it as sparingly as possible:—avoiding occasions of expence by cultivating peace, but remembering also that timely disbursements to prepare for danger frequently prevent much greater disbursements to repel it—avoiding likewise the accumulation of debt, not only by shunning occasions of expence, but by vigorous exertions in time of Peace to discharge the Debts which unavoidable wars may have occasioned, not ungenerously throwing upon posterity the burthen which we ourselves ought to bear. The execution of these maxims belongs to your Representatives, but it is necessary that public opinion should cooperate.—To facilitate to them the performance of their duty, it is essential that you should practically bear in mind, that towards the payment of debts there must be Revenue—that to have Revenue there must be taxes—that no taxes can be devised which are not more or less inconvenient and unpleasant—that the intrinsic embarrassment inseperable from the selection of the proper objects (which is always a choice of difficulties) ought to be a decisive motive for a candid construction of the conduct of the Government in making it, and for a spirit of acquiescence in the measures for obtaining Revenue which the public exigencies may at any time dictate.—

Observe good faith & justice towards all Nations. Cultivate peace and harmony with all—Religion & morality enjoin this conduct; and can it be that good policy does not equally enjoin it?—It will be worthy of a free, enlightened, and, at no distant period, a great Nation, to give to mankind the magnanimous and too novel example of a People always guided by an exalted justice & benevolence.—Who can doubt that in the course of time and things the fruits of such a plan would richly repay any temporary advantages which might be lost by a steady adherence to it? Can it be, that Providence has not coñected the permanent felicity of a Nation with its virtue?—The experiment, at least, is recommended by every sentiment which ennobles human nature.—Alas! is it rendered impossible by its vices?

In the execution of such a plan nothing is more essential than that permanent, inveterate antipathies against particular Nations and passionate attachments for others should be excluded;—and that in place of them just & amicable feelings towards all should be cultivated.—The Nation, which indulges towards another an habitual hatred, or an habitual fondness, is in some degree a slave.—It is a slave to its animosity or to its affection, either of which is sufficient to lead it astray from its duty and its interest.—Antipathy in one Nation against another—disposes each more readily to offer insult and injury, to lay hold of slight causes of umbrage, and to be haughty and intractable, when accidental or trifling occasions of dispute occur.—Hence frequent collisions, obstinate envenomed and bloody contests.—The Nation, prompted by ill will & resentment sometimes impels to War the Government, contrary to the best calculations of policy.—The Government sometimes participates in the national propensity, and adopts through passion what reason would reject;—at other times, it makes the animosity of the Nation subservient to projects of hostility instigated by pride, ambition and other sinister & pernicious motives.—The peace often, sometimes perhaps the Liberty, of Nations has been the victim.—

So likewise, a passionate attachment of one Nation for another produces a variety of evils.—Sympathy for the favourite nation, facilitating the illusion of an imaginary common interest, in cases where no real common interest exists, and infusing into one the enmities of the other, betrays the former into a participation in the quarrels & Wars of the latter, without adequate inducement or justification:—It leads also to concessions to the favourite Nation of priviledges denied to others, which is apt doubly to injure the Nation making the concessions—by unnecessarily parting with what ought to have been retained—& by exciting jealousy, ill will, and a disposition to retaliate, in the parties from whom equal priviledges are withheld: And it gives to ambitious, corrupted, or deludid citizens (who devote themselves to the favourite Nation) facility to betray, or sacrifice the interests of their own country, without odium, sometimes even with popularity;—

gilding with the apearances of a virtuous sense of obligation a commendable deference for public opinion, or a laudable zeal for public good, the base or foolish compliances of ambition corruption or infatuation.—

As avenues to foreign influence in innumerable ways, such attachments are particularly alarming to the truly enlightened and independent Patriot.—How many opportunities do they afford to tamper with domestic factions, to practise the arts of seduction, to mislead public opinion, to influence or awe the public councils!—Such an attachment of a small or weak, towards a great & powerful Nation, dooms the former to be the satellite of the latter.—

Against the insidious wiles of foreign influence, (I conjure you to believe me fellow-citizens,) the jealousy of a free people ought to be *constantly* awake; since history and experience prove that foreign influence is one of the most baneful foes of Republican Government.—But that jealousy to be useful must be impartial; else it becomes the instrument of the very influence to be avoided, instead of a defence against it.—Excessive partiality for one foreign nation and excessive dislike of another, cause those whom they actuate to see danger only on one side, and serve to veil and even second the arts of influence on the other.—Real Patriots, who may resist the intriegues of the favourite, are liable to become suspected and odious; while its tools and dupes usurp the applause & confidence of the people, to surrender their interests.—

The Great rule of conduct for us, in regard to foreign Nations is in extending our commercial relations to have with them as little *political* connection as possible.—So far as we have already formed engagements let them be fulfilled, with perfect good faith.—Here let us stop.

Europe has a set of primary interests, which to us have none, or a very remote relation.—Hence she must be engaged in frequent controversies, the causes of which are essentially foreign to our concerns. —Hence therefore it must be unwise in us to implicate ourselves, by artificial ties, in the ordinary vicissitudes of her politics, or the ordinary combinations & collisions of her friendships, or enmities:—

Our detached & distant situation invites and enables us to pursue a different course.—If we remain one People, under an efficient government, the period is not far off, when we may defy material injury from external annoyance;—when we may take such an attitude as will cause the neutrality we may at any time resolve upon to be scrupulously respected;—when belligerent nations, under the impossibility of making acquisitions upon us, will not lightly hazard the giving us provocation;—when we may choose peace or War, as our interest guided by justice shall counsel.—

Why forego the advantages of so peculiar a situation?—Why quit our own to stand upon foreign ground?—Why, by interweaving our destiny with that of any part of Europe, entangle our peace and prosperity in the toils of European Ambition, Rivalship, Interest, Humour or Caprice?—

'Tis our true policy to steer clear of permanent alliances, with any portion of the foreign world—so far, I mean, as we are now at liberty to do it—for let me not be understood as capable of patronising infidility to existing engagements (I hold the maxim no less applicable to public than to private affairs that honesty is always the best policy).—I repeat it therefore, let those engagements be observed in their genuine sense.—But in my opinion, it is unnecessary and would be unwise to extend them.—

Taking care always to keep ourselves, by suitable establishments, on a respectably defensive posture, we may safely trust to temporary alliances for extraordinary emergencies.—

Harmony, liberal intercourse with all Nations, are recommended by policy, humanity and interest.—But even our commercial policy should hold an equal and impartial hand:—neither seeking nor granting exclusive favours or preferences;—consulting the natural course of things;—diffusing & deversifying by gentle means the streams of commerce, but forcing nothing;—establishing with Powers so disposed—in order to give to trade a stable course, to define the rights of our Merchants, and to enable the Government to support them—conventional rules of intercourse; the best that present circumstances and mutual opinion will permit, but temporary, & liable to be from time to time abandoned or varied, as experience and circumstances shall dictate; constantly keeping in view, that 'tis folly in one Nation to look for disinterested favors from another—that it must pay with a portion of its Independence for whatever it may accept under that character—that by such acceptance, it may place itself in the condition of having given equivalents for nominal favours and yet of being reproached with ingratitude for not giving more.—There can be no greater error than to expect, or calculate upon real favours from Nation to Nation.—'Tis an illusion which experience must cure, which a just pride ought to discard.—

In offering to you, my Countrymen, these counsels of an old and affectionate friend, I dare not hope they will make the strong and lasting impression, I could wish—that they will controul the usual current of the passions, or prevent our Nation from running the course which has hitherto marked the Destiny of Nations:—But if I may even flatter myself, that they may be productive of some partial benefit, some occasional good;—that they may now & then recur to moderate the fury of party spirit, to warn against the mischiefs of foreign Intriegue, to guard against the Impostures of pretended patriotism—this hope will be a full recompence for the solicitude for your welfare, by which they have been dictated.—

How far in the discharge of my official duties, I have been guided by the principles which have been delineated, the public Records and other evidences of my conduct must witness to You and to the world.—To myself, the assurance of my own conscience is, that I have at least believed myself to be guided by them.

In relation to the still subsisting War in Europe, my Proclamation of the 22d of April 1793 is the index to my Plan.—Sanctioned by your approving voice and by that of Your Representatives in both Houses of Congress, the spirit of that measure has continually governed me:—uninfluenced by any attempts to deter or divert me from it.—

After deliberate examination with the aid of the best lights I could obtain I was well satisfied that our country, under all the circumstances of the case, had a right to take, and was bound in duty and interest, to take a neutral position.—Having taken it, I determined, as far as should depend upon me, to maintain it, with moderation, perseverence & firmness.—

The considerations, which respect the right to hold this conduct, it is not necessary on this occasion to detail.—I will only observe, that according to my understanding of the matter, that right, so far from being denied by any of the Belligerent Powers has been virtually admitted by all.—

The duty of holding a neutral conduct may be inferred, without any thing more, from the obligation which justice and humanity impose on every Nation, in cases in which it is free to act, to maintain inviolate the relations of Peace and amity towards other Nations.—

The inducements of interest for observing that conduct will best be referred to your own reflections & experience.—With me, a predominant motive has been to endeavour to gain time to our country to settle & mature its yet recent institutions, and to progress without interruption, to that degree of strength & consistency, which is necessary to give it, humanly speaking, the command of its own fortunes.—

Though in reviewing the incidents of my Administration, I am unconscious of intentional error—I am nevertheless too sensible of my defects not to think it probable that I may have committed many errors.—Whatever they may be I fervently beseech the Almighty to avert or mitigate the evils to which they may tend.—I shall also carry with me the hope that my Country will never cease to view them with indulgence; and that after forty five years of my life dedicated to its service, with an upright zeal, the faults of incompetent abilities will be consigned to oblivion, as myself must soon be to the mansions of rest.

Relying on its kindness in this as in other things, and actuated by that fervent love towards it, which is so natural to a man, who views in it the native soil of himself and his progenitors for several Generations; —I anticipate with pleasing expectation that retreat, in which I promise myself to realize, without alloy, the sweet enjoyment of partaking, in the midst of my fellow Citizens, the benign influence of good Laws under a free Government—the ever favourite object of my heart, and the happy reward, as I trust, of our mutual cares, labours and dangers

United States
19th September, 1796

G° WASHINGTON

LINCOLN'S SECOND INAUGURAL ADDRESS

March 4, 1865

FELLOW-COUNTRYMEN: At this second appearing to take the oath of the Presidential office, there is less occasion for an extended address than there was at the first. Then a statement somewhat in detail of a course to be pursued seemed very fitting and proper. Now, at the expiration of four years, during which public declarations have been constantly called forth on every point and phase of the great contest which still absorbs the attention and engrosses the energies of the nation, little that is new could be presented.

The progress of our arms, upon which all else chiefly depends, is as well known to the public as to myself; and it is, I trust, reasonably satisfactory and encouraging to all. With high hope for the future, no prediction in regard to it is ventured.

On the occasion corresponding to this, four years ago, all thoughts were anxiously directed to an impending civil war. All dreaded it; all sought to avoid it. While the inaugural address was being delivered from this place, devoted altogether to saving the Union without war, insurgent agents were in the city seeking to destroy it without war—seeking to dissolve the Union and divide the effects by negotiation. Both parties deprecated war; but one of them would make war rather than let the nation survive, and the other would accept war rather than let it perish; and the war came.

One eighth of the whole population were colored slaves, not distributed generally over the Union, but localized in the southern part of it. These slaves constituted a peculiar and powerful interest. All knew that this interest was somehow the cause of the war. To strengthen, perpetuate, and extend this interest, was the object for which the insurgents would rend the Union even by war, while the government claimed no right to do more than to restrict the territorial enlargement of it.

Neither party expected for the war the magnitude or the duration which it has already attained. Neither anticipated that the cause of the conflict might cease with, or even before, the conflict itself should cease. Each looked for an easier triumph, and a result less fundamental and astounding.

Both read the same Bible and pray to the same God, and each invokes his aid against the other. It may seem strange that any men should dare to ask a just God's assistance in wringing their bread from the sweat of other men's faces; but let us judge not, that we be not judged. The prayers of both could not be answered. That of neither has been answered fully. The Almighty has his own purposes. "Woe unto the world because of offenses, for it must needs be that offenses come; but woe to that man by whom the offense cometh." If we shall suppose that American slavery is one of these offenses, which in the providence of God must needs come, but which, having continued through his appointed time, he now wills to remove, and that he gives to both North and South this terrible war as the woe due to those by whom the offense came, shall we discern therein any departure from those divine attributes which the believers in a living God always ascribe to him? Fondly do we hope, fervently do we pray, that this mighty scourge of war may soon pass away. Yet, if God wills that it continue until all the wealth piled by the bondman's two hundred and fifty years of unrequited toil shall be sunk, and until every drop of blood drawn with the lash shall be paid with another drawn with the sword; as was said three thousand years ago, so still it must be said, "The judgments of the Lord are true and righteous altogether."

With malice toward none, with charity for all, with firmness in the right as God gives us to see the right, let us strive on to finish the work we are in, to bind up the nation's wounds, to care for him who shall have borne the battle and for his widow and orphans, to do all which may achieve and cherish a just and a lasting peace among ourselves and with all nations.

THE ROAD AWAY FROM REVOLUTION

BY WOODROW WILSON

In these doubtful and anxious days, when all the world is at unrest, and, look which way you will, the road ahead seems darkened by shadows which portend dangers of many kinds, it is only common prudence that we should look about us and attempt to assess the causes of distress and the most likely means of removing them.

There must be some real ground for the universal unrest and perturbation. It is not to be found in superficial politics or in mere economic blunders. It probably lies deep at the sources of the spiritual life of our time. It leads to revolution; and perhaps if we take the case of the Russian Revolution, the outstanding event of its kind in our age, we may find a good deal of instruction for our judgment of present critical situations and circumstances.

What gave rise to the Russian Revolution? The answer can only be that it was the product of a whole social system. It was not, in fact, a sudden thing. It had been gathering head for several generations. It was due to the systematic denial to the great body of Russians of the rights and privileges which all normal men desire and must have if they are to be contented and within reach of happiness. The lives of the great mass of the Russian people contained no opportunities, but were hemmed in by barriers against which they were constantly flinging their spirits, only to fall back bruised and dispirited. Only the powerful were suffered to secure their rights or even to gain access to the means of material success.

It is to be noted as a leading fact of our time that it was against "capitalism" that the Russian leaders directed their attack. It was capitalism that made them see red; and it is against capitalism under one name or another that the discontented classes everywhere draw their indictment.

There are thoughtful and well-informed men all over the world who believe, with much apparently sound reason, that the abstract thing, the system, which we call capitalism, is indispensable to the industrial support and development of modern civilization. And yet everyone who has an intelligent knowledge of social forces must know that great and widespread reactions like that which is now unquestionably manifesting itself against capitalism do not occur without cause or provocation; and before we commit ourselves irreconcilably to an attitude of hostility to this movement of the time, we ought frankly to put to ourselves the question, Is the capitalistic system unimpeachable? which is another way of asking, Have capitalists generally used their power for the benefit of the countries in which their capital is employed and for the benefit of their fellow men?

Is it not, on the contrary, too true that capitalists have often seemed to regard the men whom they used as mere instruments of profit, whose physical and mental powers it was legitimate to exploit with as slight cost to themselves as possible, either of money or of sympathy? Have not many fine men who were actuated by the highest principles in every other relationship of life seemed to hold that generosity and humane feeling were not among the imperative mandates of conscience in the conduct of a banking business, or in the development of an industrial or commercial enterprise?

And, if these offenses against high morality and true citizenship have been frequently observable, are we to say that the blame for the present discontent and turbulence is wholly on the side of those who are in revolt against them? Ought we not, rather, to seek a way to remove such offenses and make life itself clean for those who will share honorably and cleanly in it?

The world has been made safe for democracy. There need now be no fear that any such mad design as that entertained by the insolent and ignorant Hohenzollerns and their counselors may prevail against it. But democracy has not yet made the world safe against irrational revolution. That supreme task, which is nothing less than the salvation of civilization, now faces democracy, insistent, imperative. There is no escaping it, unless everything we have built up is presently to fall in ruin about us; and the United States, as the greatest of democracies, must undertake it.

The road that leads away from revolution is clearly marked, for it is defined by the nature of men and of organized society. It therefore behooves us to study very carefully and very candidly the exact nature of the task and the means of its accomplishment.

The nature of men and of organized society dictates the maintenance in every field of action of the highest and purest standards of justice and of right dealing; and it is essential to efficacious thinking in this critical matter that we should not entertain a narrow or technical conception of justice. By justice the lawyer generally means the prompt, fair, and open application of impartial rules; but we call ours a Christian civilization, and a Christian conception of justice must be much higher. It must include sympathy and helpfulness and a willingness to forgo self-interest in order to promote the welfare, happiness, and contentment of others and of the community as a whole. This is what our age is blindly feeling after in its reaction against what it deems the too great selfishness of the capitalistic system.

The sum of the whole matter is this, that our civilization cannot survive materially unless it be redeemed spiritually. It can be saved only by becoming permeated with the spirit of Christ and being made free and happy by the practices which spring out of that spirit. Only thus can discontent be driven out and all the shadows lifted from the road ahead.

Here is the final challenge to our churches, to our political organizations, and to our capitalists—to everyone who fears God or loves his country. Shall we not all earnestly co-operate to bring in the new day?

DOUGLAS MacARTHUR'S ADDRESS AT THE FORMAL SURRENDER OF JAPAN ON BOARD THE U.S. BATTLESHIP *MISSOURI*

September 2, 1945

THE FORMALITIES OF THE SURRENDER

We are gathered here, representatives of the major warring powers, to conclude a solemn agreement whereby Peace may be restored. The issues, involving divergent ideals and ideologies, have been determined on the battle fields of the world and hence are not for our discussion or debate. Nor is it for us here to meet, representing as we do a majority of the peoples of the Earth, in a spirit of distrust, malice or hatred. But rather it is for us, both victors and vanquished, to rise to that higher dignity which alone befits the sacred purposes we are about to serve, committing all of our peoples unreservedly to faithful compliance with the undertakings they are here formally to assume.

It is my earnest hope and indeed the hope of all mankind that from this solemn occasion a better world shall emerge out of the blood and carnage of the past—a world founded upon faith and understanding —a world dedicated to the dignity of man and the fulfillment of his most cherished wish—for freedom, tolerance and justice.

The terms and conditions upon which surrender of the Japanese Imperial forces is here to be given and accepted are contained in the instrument of surrender now before you.

As Supreme Commander for the Allied Powers I announce it my firm purpose, in the tradition of the countries I represent, to proceed in the discharge of my responsibilities with justice and tolerance, while taking all necessary dispositions to insure that the terms of surrender are fully, promptly and faithfully complied with.

I now invite the representatives of the Emperor of Japan and the Japanese Government, and the Japanese Imperial General Headquarters to sign the instrument of surrender at the places indicated.

The Supreme Commander for the Allied Powers will now sign on behalf of all the Nations at war with Japan.

The representative of the United States of America will now sign.

The representative of the Republic of China will now sign.

The representative of the United Kingdom will now sign.

The representative of the Union of Soviet Socialist Republics will now sign.

The representative of Australia will now sign.

The representative of Canada will now sign.

The representative of France will now sign.

The representative of Netherlands will now sign.

The representative of New Zealand will now sign.

Let us pray that Peace be now restored to the world, and that God will preserve it always. These proceedings are closed.

The Address

My fellow countrymen:

Today the guns are silent. A great tragedy has ended. A great victory has been won. The skies no longer rain death—the seas bear only commerce—men everywhere walk upright in the sunlight. The entire world lies quietly at Peace. The Holy Mission has been completed. And in reporting this to you, the people, I speak for the thousands of silent lips, forever stilled among the jungles and the beaches and in the deep waters of the Pacific which marked the way. I speak for the unnamed brave millions homeward bound to take up the challenge of that future which they did so much to salvage from the brink of disaster.

As I look back on the long, tortuous trail from those grim days of Bataan and Corregidor, when an entire world lived in fear; when Democracy was on the defensive everywhere, when modern civilization trembled in the balance, I thank a merciful God that He has given us the faith, the courage and the power from which to mould victory. We have known the bitterness of defeat and the exultation of triumph, and from both we have learned there can be no turning back. We must go forward to preserve in Peace what we won in War.

A new era is upon us. Even the lesson of Victory itself brings with it profound concern, both for our future security and the survival of civilization. The destructiveness of the War potential, through progressive advances in scientific discovery, has in fact now reached a point which revises the traditional concept of War.

Men since the beginning of time have sought peace. Various methods through the ages have been attempted to devise an international process to prevent or settle disputes between nations. From the very start workable methods were found in so far as individual citizens were concerned but the mechanics of an instrumentality of larger international scope have never been successful. Military alliances, balance of power, Leagues of Nations all in turn failed leaving the only path to be by the way of the crucible of war. The utter destructiveness of war now blots out this alternative. We have had our last chance. If we do not devise some greater and more equitable system Armageddon will be at our door. The problem basically is theological and involves a spiritual recrudescence and improvement of human character that will synchronize with our almost matchless advance in science, art, literature and all material and cultural developments of the past two thousand years. It must be of the spirit if we are to save the flesh.

We stand in Tokyo today reminiscent of our countryman, Commodore Perry, ninety-two years ago. His purpose was to bring to Japan an era of enlightenment and progress by lifting the veil of isolation to the friendship, trade and commerce of the world. But alas the knowledge thereby gained of Western science was forged into an instrument of oppression and human enslavement. Freedom of expression, freedom of action, even freedom of thought were denied through suppression of liberal education, through appeal to superstition and through the application of force. We are committed by the Potsdam Declaration of Principles to see that the Japanese people are liberated from this condition of slavery. It is my purpose to implement this commitment just as rapidly as the armed forces are demobilized and other essential steps taken to neutralize the war potential. The energy of the Japanese race, if properly directed, will enable expansion vertically rather than horizontally. If the talents of the race are turned into constructive channels, the country can lift itself from its present deplorable state into a position of dignity.

To the Pacific basin has come the vista of a new emancipated world. Today, freedom is on the offensive, democracy is on the march. Today, in Asia as well as in Europe, unshackled peoples are tasting the full sweetness of liberty, the relief from fear.

In the Philippines, America has evolved a model for this new free world of Asia. In the Philippines, America has demonstrated that peoples of the East and peoples of the West may walk side by side in mutual respect and with mutual benefit. The history of our sovereignty there has now the full confidence of the East.

And so, my fellow countrymen, today I report to you that your sons and daughters have served you well and faithfully, with the calm, deliberate, determined fighting spirit of the American soldier and sailor based upon a tradition of historical truth, as against the fanaticism of an enemy supported only by mythological fiction. Their spiritual strength and power has brought us through to victory. They are homeward bound—take care of them.

A PUBLISHER'S APPRECIATION

In the preparation of this volume THE LONG HOUSE has conferred and corresponded with a number of men and women whose unfailing consideration and cooperation have made the task a pleasure and association with them an honor. We would like to thank them again, this time publicly.

They are:

Hon. August E. Johansen, of Winter Park, Florida; Dr. Philip P. Brower, Director, Bureau of Archives, of the MacArthur Memorial in Norfolk, Virginia; and Major General Courtney Whitney, aide to General MacArthur, who participated so generously in the search which finally resulted in the first publication of General MacArthur's preparatory Notes for his *Missouri* address.

Mrs. Robert H. McCauley, Jr., Curator of Graphics of the Maryland Historical Society in Baltimore, for her work, on behalf of the Society, in supplying us with copies of the original manuscripts of Francis Scott Key.

Mr. Charles G. Muller, of Westport, Connecticut, for the verification of certain incidents surrounding the composing of *The Star-Spangled Banner*, and which he had substantiated during the writing of his own book, *The Darkest Day.*

Mr. David C. Mearns, of Washington, D.C., former Chief of the Manuscripts Division of The Library of Congress, gentleman, scholar and friend.

Mr. John C. Broderick, in 1968 the Acting Chief of the Manuscripts Division of the Library, who so ably is carrying on the tradition established by Mr. Mearns.

The Reverend Robert F. Williams, of Whittier, California, for his deep understanding and appreciation of the intrinsic beauties of the philosophy of the true American, and for his friendship.

The excerpts of Washington's Farewell Address have been reproduced by courtesy of the Manuscripts Division, The New York Public Library, Astor, Lenox and Tilden Foundations.

The manuscript, and first sheet music, of *The Star-Spangled Banner* are from the Collections of the Maryland Historical Society.

abolishing our most ~~important~~ valuable Laws

for taking away our charters & altering fundamentally the forms of our govern

for suspending our own legislatures & declaring themselves invested with powe

legislate for us in all cases whatsoever:

he has abdicated government here, [by declaring us out of his protection & waging war against] [withdrawing his governors, & declaring us

of his allegiance & protection:]

he has plundered our seas, ravaged our coasts, burnt our towns & destroyed

lives of our people:

he is at this time transporting large armies of [Scotch and other] foreign mercenaries to comp

the works of death, desolation & tyranny already begun with circumstances

[scarcely paralleled in the most barbarous ages & totally]

of cruelty & perfidy unworthy the head of a civilized nation:

he has endeavored to bring on the inhabitants of our frontiers the merciless Ind

savages, whose known rule of warfare is an undistinguished destructio

all ages, sexes, & conditions [of existence:]

he has incited treasonable insurrections of our fellow-~~citizens~~, with t

allurements of forfeiture & confiscation of our property:

[he has constrained others ... on the high seas to bear arms against their country ... to become the executioners of their friends & brethren]

he has waged cruel war against human nature itself, violating it's most

cred rights of life & liberty in the persons of a distant people who never

fended him, captivating & carrying them into slavery in another hemi

sphere, or to incur miserable death in their transportation thither. th

piratical warfare, the opprobrium of infidel powers, is the warfare of

Christian king of Great Britain. determined to keep open a marke

where MEN should be bought & sold he has prostituted his negati

for suppressing every legislative attempt to prohibit or to restrain this

~~determining to keep open a market where MEN should be bought & sold~~

execrable commerce; and that this assemblage of horrors might want no f

of distinguished die, he is now exciting those very people to rise in arm

among us, and to purchase that liberty of which he has deprived th

by murdering the people upon whom he also obtruded them: thus pay

off former crimes committed against the liberties of one people, with crim

which he urges them to commit against the lives of another.]

in every stage of these oppressions we have petitioned for redress in the most hum

terms; our repeated petitions have been answered only by repeated injuries. a prin

whose character is thus marked by every act which may define a tyrant, is un

to be the ruler of a free people [who mean to be free. future ages will scarce belie

that the hardiness of one man, adventured within the short compass of twelve yea

to build a foundation so broad & undisguised, for tyranny

only, ~~[illegible]~~ over a people fostered & fixed in princ

of ~~liberty~~ freedom.]